# Unpacking Depth Sport Psychology



This book utilizes a wealth of case studies to demonstrate the importance of using depth sport psychology to explore the athletes' unconscious feelings and fears, and provides the knowledge needed to help athletes deal with pressures.

Applying the theories of Sigmund Freud, Alfred Adler, Carl Jung, Margaret Mahler, Melanie Klein, Heinz Kohut, Donald Winnicott, and Christopher Bollas to explain the athlete's mind, this useful resource will help develop a better understanding of athlete's repressed feelings and psychological states. It looks past the cognitive behavioural techniques currently used to aid athletes, and instead focuses on the many ways the unconscious subtly influences athletes, offering an important paradigm shift. Covering a range of different athletes within various sports, each chapter demonstrates how the psychoanalytic techniques of free association, the working alliance, analytic interpretations, confrontation, dream analysis, transference/counter transference and resistance analysis are used with athletes. Case studies cover such topics as the treatment of anxiety, yips, anger, guilt and perfectionism in the athlete, the influence of birth order, psychological defences used by athletes including gamesmanship, dissociation and humor, and the psychology of injury.

Unpacking Depth Sport Psychology is the ideal resource for students, the educated athlete, parents, professors, sport psychologists, and coaches who hope to improve the athletes' performance.

Dr. **Tom Ferraro** is a psychoanalyst and sport psychologist living in New York, USA and working with professional athletes, Olympians, and professional teams in a variety of sports. In addition, he is an award-winning writer whose work has been featured in *The New York Times, The Times* (UK), and *The Wall Street Journal* and is a frequent guest on national television shows.

# Unpacking Depth Sport Psychology

## Case Studies in the Unconscious

**Tom Ferraro**

Routledge
Taylor & Francis Group
NEW YORK AND LONDON

Designed cover image: © Getty Images

First published 2023
by Routledge
605 Third Avenue, New York, NY 10158

and by Routledge
4 Park Square, Milton Park, Abingdon, Oxon OX14 4RN

*Routledge is an imprint of the Taylor & Francis Group, an informa business*



*Library of Congress Cataloging-in-Publication Data*
A catalog record for this title has been requested

ISBN: 978-1-032-22407-7 (hbk)
ISBN: 978-1-032-22404-6 (pbk)
ISBN: 978-1-003-27246-5 (ebk)

DOI: 10.4324/9781003272465

Typeset in Bembo
by Taylor & Francis Books

This book is dedicated to every athlete who has missed a three-foot putt, double faulted on the tennis court, popped a jump in figure skating, hesitated before shooting the puck, yipped on the mound, dropped an easy pass in football, or feared a back flip on the balance beam. Be very proud of who you are because you are the heroes of our world, the ones who were not afraid to step into the batter's box and face the next pitch as well as "the roar of the greasepaint and the smell of the crowd." You all have my admiration and respect.

# Contents

PART III
**Case Studies of Depressed Athletes** 57



PART IV
**Case Studies of How Athletes Use Psychological Defenses** 71



PART V
**Case Studies of The Way Birth Order Influences an Athlete's Performance** 101

# Preface

In its current state, sport psychology is failing the athlete and threatens to become little more than a well-meaning hoax. As a sport psychologist myself, it pains me to write this, and I authored this book because no one else would. There are increasing numbers of athletes who see the importance of mental conditioning but are given meaningless mantras rather than a chance to explore their history and their unconscious conflicts. They quickly learn that shallow interventions which only skim the surface do little to help them resolve their yips or their slumps. Cognitive behavior modification has dominated the field of sport psychology for the past 70 years, and its practitioners were certainly not going to write about how it has failed the athlete. And except for a few practitioners, psychoanalysts have shown a remarkable lack of interest in sports. Which meant I would have to write this book myself.

Authoring a book is a daunting affair. In response to the question of how you write a novel, Ernest Hemingway said "Well, I begin by defrosting the refrigerator." This comment reveals both the need to avoid the arduous task of writing a 65,000-word text and the need to thaw one's anxiety in order to begin. When faced with the challenge of maintaining the reader's interest for an entire book, I felt frozen, much like the case of an Olympic sprinter you will read about who became frozen in the blocks at the Olympic Trials. I worked my way through my book writing block by telling myself to relax and just have fun with each chapter. This strategy is one I try to teach athletes when they tell me they are overwhelmed, and this concept is elaborated in the chapter about the basketball player.

In truth, the journey to this book began when I was a teenage golfer with grandiose dreams of playing on the tour, a dream which dissolved the day I played a match against a young Ben Crenshaw who beat me easily, whereupon I developed a keen interest in my second career choice, to be a psychologist. In college, I continued to play Division I golf, and after graduation, I was accepted into the Ph.D. Program at SUNY Stony Brook, with a faculty that included some of the founders of behavior therapy. Upon graduation from SUNY Stony Brook, I worked in a clinic that did cutting-edge behavior modification on severely ill obsessive compulsives, and it was there that I realized that even vigorously applied cutting-edge behavior modification will only ameliorate some of the patient's symptoms with no guarantee that the symptoms wouldn't return. In addition, the patients wanted more than just symptom relief and wanted to actually learn something about themselves. This prompted me to return for four more years of analytic training which included about 2,400 hours of personal therapy. As I set up my private practice, I had never lost my passion for sports and reached out to athletes I knew, offering my services. Initially I provided them with behavioral interventions in the hope that this would be sufficient to help them get over the yips, poor focus, anger issues and slumps. However, I came to realize that behavioral interventions were of limited value in the face of intense competitive pressure and I saw that psychoanalytic theory offered the widest array of interventions robust enough to manage an athlete's extreme stress.

So here we are. What you are about to read is a text that explains through case studies how psychoanalysis works with athletes and their performance woes. The 32 cases you will read are based upon my analytic work with professional and Olympic level athletes from a variety of sports. This book is a call for a paradigm shift in sport psychology which finally addresses the most crucial area in an athlete's life, their own unconscious which turns out to be, by far, their toughest opponent.

There are many professors, psychoanalysts, editors, friends and loved ones who helped me along the way. Dr. Herb Kaye, Ph.D. at SUNY Stony Brook, Dr. George Nicklin, M.D. at the Long Island Institute of Psychoanalysis, Steven Blank of Blank Slate Media, Bob Carney, senior editor of Golf Digest, Dr. David Burston, Ph.D. of the English Premier League, Dr. Christopher Bollas, Ph.D. for all his encouragement, and illustrator Hye Ryun Hong, M.S. for her support and laughter and to Maddie Gray, my kind and steadfast editor at Routledge.

# 1 Prologue

> "A discipline is mature only insofar as it is capable of 'undergoing' a crisis in all of its basic concepts and procedures"
>
> (Heidegger, Being and Time)

## 1 The Freudian Playbook

The purpose of this chapter is to introduce the theories and techniques of psychoanalysis as applied to athletes and their performance issues. With very few exceptions, the unconscious of the athlete has yet to be explored. Most sport psychology textbooks are heavily oriented toward cognitive behaviorism which has long had a systemic denial of the unconscious. Conversely, psychoanalysts have not regarded sport as a legitimate area of study, even though sport is one of culture's primary forms of sublimation. The theories of the unconscious were first developed by Freud and expanded upon in the Object Relations and Self-Psychology Schools, and each may be of value in specific athletic situations. The argument will be made that the cognitive behavioral paradigm now in favor, is ineffective because it denies the existence of the athletes' unconscious whereas psychoanalytic theories posit that the unconscious exists and has the ultimate say on the outcome of games and athletic careers. A psychoanalytic approach allows the athlete to seek and face the buried traumas of their past.

A change in basic assumptions is needed in sport psychology since much of the athlete's problems remain unconscious where standard cognitive behavioral techniques do not penetrate. Psychodynamic psychotherapy is well equipped to address these underlying and often intractable problems.

As Thomas Kuhn explained in "The Structure of Scientific Revolutions," most fields of science become lodged within one paradigm based upon a single scientific discovery. This paradigm becomes self-reinforcing and self-perpetuating despite its significant limitations. When a competing paradigm emerges, it is initially resisted but eventually the field accommodates to this new paradigm and establishes a new set of assumptions. This is the way

DOI: 10.4324/9781003272465-1

science grows and this is what is about to happen in sport psychology over the next decade. (Kuhn, 1962).

Sport is a carefully measured public performance where the stress of confrontation cannot be avoided. The question of glory or shame is felt at every moment. Competitive sports elicit extremes of anxiety, anger, despair, shame, excitement, and pride, and because of this, sport psychology has emerged as a field designed to help. If these intense emotions are not mastered, the athlete will fail.

Sports embraced cognitive behavioral techniques, because it offered the promise of quick-fix easy to master solutions to complex emotional problems. The stakes are high in big time sports, and there is always a push for swift answers. The fact that these interventions have extremely limited effectiveness did not seem to matter much. Coaches and owners were blinded by hope which prompted the naïve belief that positive psychology pep talks would do the trick. However, they have begun to realize that quick fixes are not forthcoming. It mattered little whether one used Joseph Wolpe's theory of reciprocal inhibition or systematic desensitization, (Wolpe, 1958), Aaron Beck's cognitive therapy (Beck and Emery, 1985) or Al Bandura's efficacy theory (Bandura, 1977) because all of these approaches were destined to fail by ignoring the underlying unconscious dynamics which continued to exert influence on performance.

Shallow solutions to complex athletic problems are like taking a pain killer when you have cancer. The medicine may give temporary relief, but the cancer continues to grow. Expecting a positive self-talk mantra to help a stressed-out Olympic athlete is comparable to building a sandcastle on the beach and expecting it to stop an incoming tsunami.

Real cure takes time and effort. Trust must be established, defenses must be modified, resistance overcome, an observing ego must be created, insights into the underlying unconscious issues must be seen and mastered. This is not easy, and it is not quick.

There has always been fear and antagonism toward Sigmund Freud and psychoanalysis because most people sense that the cure will be painful. The character of psychiatrist Hannibal Lector in the film "Silence of the Lambs" is an example of just how terrified most people are of the psychoanalyst's gaze. The moment I am introduced as a psychoanalyst at a party or when playing golf, the friendly banter stops, and silence ensues.

The fear of facing the unconscious led the way to the field of behaviorism beginning with B. F. Skinner (1938), John Watson (1924), Pavlov (1928), and Hans Eysenck (1947.) Their theories focused exclusively on observable behavior in contrast to psychoanalysis, which based most of its interventions on unconscious processes.

Although classical conditioning was helpful in animal training, over time it became obvious that humans were more complex than lab rats and by the 1960s Aaron Beck instigated the cognitive revolution which introduced the Second Wave in psychotherapy. Beck (1975), Albert Ellis (1962) and others suggested that man was more than a mass of robotic behaviors and that we had an active mind inside of us. Slowly, behaviorism morphed into cognitive behavior therapy and 'acceptance therapy' (Hayes, Strosahl, and Wilson, 1999) where it remains to this day, a discipline boxed within a mechanistic and hyper-rationalist approach. Farhad Dalal's book "CBT: The Cognitive Behavioral Tsunami" (2018) reviews these developments in detail.

Cognitive behavioral sport psychology focused upon anxiety and anger, thereby ignoring a variety of more subtle affects in sports including envy, shame, guilt, greed, and self-defeat. This leaves the embattled athlete to fend for themselves regarding these more subtle and deep-rooted affects. Furthermore, the evidence regarding the efficacy of cognitive behavior therapy in treating either anxiety or anger is sparse, biased, and unpersuasive (Dalal, 2018, Gardner and Moore, 2005).

The mechanistic approach of cognitive behavior sport psychology has placed the field at an arid impasse, and the question that remains is which other theoretical approach will help the field to grow. The techniques of psychoanalysis have a long history of treating a wide variety of affects including shame, depression, guilt, envy, jealousy, and self-defeat, and therefore it is a discipline uniquely equipped to take sport psychology to the next level. Psychoanalysis remains unrivaled in its attention to resistance, regression, acting out, and other unconscious defenses that many athletes are prone to and in addition it is a more humanistic approach which emphasizes the uniqueness of each case.

Any sport psychologist working with professional athletes soon realizes that the suppressive devices used in cognitive/behavioral psychology have minimal effectiveness (Gardner and Moore, 2006.) Behavioral therapy is based upon an impressive model of learning theory, but the reinforcement protocols and the suppressive techniques used by cognitive behavioral sport psychologists don't seem to hold back the intense internal and external pressures that are regularly elicited by sports.

Psychoanalysts believe the answers to the athlete's immature defenses, character flaws, and neurotic performance problems are found in their past. From birth to age six, parents and siblings have a major impact on identity. This is followed by experiences in middle school and high school which cement earlier identity. This early childhood identity acts as a shadow to everything experienced later in life, including mood, perceptions, ability to learn, motivation, behavior, and self- esteem. These experiences remain embedded in our unconscious, and Freud was the first to elaborate this and over the past 120 years his theories and techniques have been expanded and clarified. His theories have had a significant impact on literature, advertising, business, art, dance, and film. Yet Freud's theory of the id, ego, and super ego has had virtually no impact on the field of sport psychology. This is not because the athlete does not need help in these areas but because sport psychologists did not pursue the added four years of training required to become psychoanalysts.

The power of denial and reaction formation is seen in the very first chapter of one of the most popular sport psychology books in print by one of the world's most popular sport psychologists. His first chapter is entitled "On MY Interpretation of Dreams" and it begins like this:

> "I have two things in common with Sigmund Freud. I have a couch in my consulting room. And I ask people to tell me about their dreams. But there the resemblance ends."

He suggests that Freud's theory encourages athletes to think of themselves as victims of their past and goes on to boldly state that the psychology of great golf is quite plain and amazingly simple and the players he works with are amazed by the simplicity of what he tells them. (Rotella, 1995.) The fact that he begins his book with references to Freud suggests that his judgment may be influenced by the defenses of denial, reaction formation, fear, and envy, and I doubt that Dr. Rotella has been analyzed and helped to work through these issues.

Indeed, simplicity sells well, as any Hollywood producer will tell you, but the reality is that an athlete's unconscious is complex, mysterious, hard to penetrate and has the final word on whether an athlete performs well or not. Sport psychology currently derides the idea of an unconscious and assumes that short term techniques that focus on symptom relief with visualization, relaxation tips, and positive self-talk, are going to help solve the embedded conflicts and confusions that lie within the unconscious. Often this model amounts to not much more than "Don't worry, be happy."

Professional coaches are by now aware of the triviality of self-talk tips. I was once asked by a coach of a professional soccer team I was working with "Don't tell me you're going to teach my team to untie, and they re-tie their shoes to make their anger go away?"

Every elite athlete I have known has been exposed to the full gamut of mental skill training through team meetings and at academies where a sport psychologist has been brought in to teach a few seminars on visualization, positive self-talk, focus techniques, and relaxation methods. And now with the availability of YouTube and podcasts, nearly all athletes have perused the internet in hope of finding that magical tip to dissolve their anxiety and obliterate their habits of self-defeat. However, the ingrained patterns of self-defeat remain untouched and in control.

A good example of just how blind athletes are to their own unconscious problems is seen in the life of Tiger Woods. One must ask how on earth anyone can be so oblivious to the dangers of scandal, paparazzi, and prostitutes. His naivety was summarily shattered the moment that his wife, Elin Nordegren, hit him in the mouth with his nine iron after she discovered his womanizing ways. His acting out behavior was labeled as a 'sex addiction', which is like saying alcoholism is best explained by saying booze tastes good. The reality is that the unconscious of Tiger Woods was in charge, and it cost him about

$700 million in lost endorsements. Such is the potent self-destructive power of the unconscious. Whether Tiger Woods felt empty, angry, entitled or wished to be out of his high-pressured sporting life, one can safely assume that he was largely unaware of these dynamics and therefore vulnerable to acting them out in self-destructive, costly and counterproductive ways.

Rather than getting real help, the athlete will often choose superstitious behavior, acting out, psychosomatic illness, injury, self-medication, or 30-day rehabs to suppress their symptoms of anger, exhaustion, anxiety, guilt, tension, sleeplessness, depression, grief or inner conflict.

In this book I will make the case that depth sport psychology is uniquely equipped to deal with the gravity and complexity of the problems and pressures felt by the athlete, their coaches, and general managers. My methods come under the heading of long-term psychodynamic psychotherapy, and there are very few trained psychoanalysts working full time in the field at present. There is Dr. David Burston who works with the English Premier League in London, Mark Nesti of the English Premier League and Dr. Marcelo M. Suarez-Orozco and Dr. Rubenstein both of whom treat soccer players in South America. I am working in New York with tennis players, soccer stars, PGA Tour golfers, MLB pitchers, football players in the NFL, basketball players in the WNBA, MMA fighters, gymnasts, and figure skaters.

I will be presenting cases from my practice with world renowned athletes to explore the way their unconscious dictates the arc of their career. When the unconscious goes untreated, it produces anxiety, underperformance, despair, poor focus, drug use, costly slumps, and injury, and at times it brings a career to an early end. I will change critical details of each player to make it impossible to accurately identify the player in question and to insure anonymity.

I will introduce psychoanalytic theories in chapter one and follow this with a chapter on techniques including the working alliance, creating the framework, free association, dream analysis, resistance analysis, transference, and counter transference. I will then present cases from the world of track and field, golf, tennis, hockey, baseball, basketball, figure skating, swimming, boxing, Jiu jitsu, bowling, and lacrosse. I will be discussing the athlete's fears, anxieties, yips, anger, accident proneness, exhaustion, envy, jealousy, and lapses of focus. I will also discuss emotions like shame, guilt, overcompensation, burnout, perfectionism, psychotic breaks, and the psychology behind injuries.

It is my hope and intention to give the reader a feel for the challenge, complexity, excitement, and great pleasure it is to work with athletes using a psychoanalytic approach.

## References

Bandura, A. (1977) Self-Efficacy: Toward a unifying theory of behavioral change. *Psychology Review*, 84, 191–215.

Beck, A. (1975) *Cognitive Therapy and the Emotional Disorders*. International Universities Press.

Beck, A. and Emery, G. (1985) *Anxiety disorders and phobias: A cognitive perspective*. Basic Books.

Dalal, F. (2018) *CBT: the Cognitive Behavioral Tsunami*. Routledge.

Ellis, A. (1962) *Reason and Emotion in Psychotherapy*. Lyle Stuart.

Eysenck, H. (1947) *Dimensions of Personality*. Routledge and Kegan Paul.

Freud, S. (1900) *The Interpretation of Dreams* (Translated into English in 1913). Macmillan.

Gardner, F. and Moore, Z. (2005) *Clinical Sport Psychology*. Human Kinetics.

Hayes, S, Strosahl, K., and Wilson, K. (1999) *Acceptance and Commitment Therapy*. The Guilford Press.

Kuhn, T. (1962) *The Structure of Scientific Revolutions*. The University of Chicago Press.

Pavlov, I, (1928) *Conditioned Reflexes, An investigation of the physiological activities of the cerebral cortex*. Oxford University Press.

Rotella, B. (1995) *Golf is not a Game of Perfect*. Simon & Schuster.

Skinner, B. F. (1938) *The Behavior of Organisms; An Experimental Analysis*. Appleton-Century.

Watson, J. (1924) *Behaviorism*. University of Chicago Press.

Wolpe, J. (1958) *Psychotherapy by reciprocal inhibition*. Stanford University Press.

# 2 Psychoanalytic Theories Applied to Athletes

"Flectere si nequeo superos, Acheronta movebo"
(If I cannot bend the Higher Powers, I will move the nether regions)
Freud, 1900

There are several psychoanalytic theories that clarify the athlete's performance problems. Most of these theories have not been applied to the field of sports. In this chapter I will describe how each theory can be used to treat athletes who are anxious or self-defeating. Psychoanalysts believe that athletes have an unconscious and that psychological defenses have been established to deal with painful memories, taboo urges, or conflicts. These issues must be uncovered and worked through to escape repeating patterns of self-defeat.

"The Divine Comedy" by Dante Alighieri is a story about a depressed man, lost in the woods and wishing to find happiness. He sees an easy way out of the woods and rushes towards it, only to be blocked by wild beasts. The poet Virgil appears and informs him that the only way out of his depression is to go down through the circles of hell and face his demons head on. Although written 570 years before Freud, this classic of Western literature reveals the philosophy of psychoanalysis which is that a patient must face their inner demons before growth can be achieved.

Psychoanalysis with athletes emphasizes an understanding of the causes of problems rather than making an immediate attempt at suppression. Athletes tend to favor action over understanding, and many are alexithymic and explains why cognitive behavioral techniques, which emphasize suppression have been favored. But no matter how conscientiously one applies positive psychology mantras, they will have little short-term or long-term impact on athletic performance.

So let us introduce some of the major psychoanalytic theories and provide a rationale for why they may be useful to athletes and the practitioners who treat them.

**Sigmund Freud's theory of Id, Ego, and Super Ego**: Freud is the founder of psychoanalysis, and his theory of the unconscious has had profound influence on psychotherapy as well as literature, film criticism, behavioral economics, art, art criticism, theater, and psychohistory. Psychoanalysis posits that a significant portion of human motivation, behavior, and outcomes, and

DOI: 10.4324/9781003272465-2

this includes sports behavior, are dictated by unconscious forces that we are not aware of. While our conscious mind may desire a win, our unconscious mind may desire a loss. According to Freud, the human psyche consists of three components, the id, the ego and the super ego (S. Freud, 1923).

**The Id:** The Id is the repository of our instinctual drives, repressed memories, and past traumas. Freud suggested that the Id was part of our primary animal nature. Our ego or consciousness has little awareness of our Id, and its instinctual needs. The Id contains both our sexual and aggressive drives. Our desire to experience pleasure is expressed with sex, by eating or sublimated into artistic or sports activities. Our aggressive instinct to dominate, destroy and to kill is the other aspect of our instinctual life and is expressed through war, business competition, and sublimated sports activities. The world of sports is compelling because it directly taps into our pleasure seeking and our aggressive drives and converts them into something pro social, safe, and enjoyable. Each sport provides a different balance for our drives. Sports such as gymnastics, figure skating and soccer sublimate sexual instincts a bit more clearly whereas sports like boxing, football, fencing, and hockey rely more on our aggressive urges to kill or destroy (Suarez-Orozco, 1999).

**The Superego:** The Superego consists of the internalized rules and standards which serve to keep us in check and within normal limits of acceptability. As an example, an athlete with a very harsh super ego has overly high standards and will be chronically angry with himself after any mistake. In contrast, an athlete with a more reasonable super ego will accept mistakes more readily. A harsh superego often leads to slumps as the athlete harangues himself and suffers chronic disappointment. An overly harsh superego must be softened and resolved for these slumps to be avoided. This is one of the ways the superego has an impact on performance. Case studies will be used to explain this aspect of the mind in detail.

**The Ego:** The ego or our conscious mind serves as a mediator between our primitive desires and our ethical standards. The Ego does not function with free will as the behavior modifiers believe (Rotella, 1995) but rather must choose many compromise positions to deal with inner drives and the guilt feelings they produce. Athletes who have grown up with inadequate parenting or who are spoiled, develop a weak super ego which will lead to either sociopathy or narcissism. Athletes with weak super egos often make headlines by committing crimes with O. J. Simpson as the best example. Sociopathic athletes with weak super egos are a nightmare for any sports organization. The compromise between the athlete's instinctual desires and their enfeebled judgement is problematic and often they make career ending mistakes. Athletes who have had adequate parenting and thereby good consciences have little trouble managing most of the rules in sports and in society and are not bogged down by rule breaking tendencies. Case studies of athletes who lack super ego function and are crippled with sociopathy and narcissism will be discussed and how changes in the Id and Super Ego lead to greater ego strength and executive function.

Freud's theories are contained in the more than 60 books that he wrote during his long career, and they serve as the foundation of psychoanalysis and psychotherapy. He was responsible for the uncovering of the unconscious and the necessity of exploring it to effect a cure. His mandate was "where Id was, let there be Ego" which means that where unconscious feelings exist, let them be transformed by words. This takes place over an extended period, and we will be referring to his work throughout this book and in nearly every case study presented.

**Alfred Adler's theory of overcompensation:** Alfred Adler was a founding member of psychoanalysis along with Freud and Jung and is known for his concepts of the inferiority complex, overcompensation, and birth order effects (Adler, 1964). Adler believed that feelings of smallness as a child created the need to overcompensate for this internal sense of inferiority and is the source of our drive to win. His theory is well suited to the study of the type of elite athlete who has a chip on his shoulder and has something to prove. The chapter on the Will to Win will show the use of Adler's theory of overcompensation.

**Carl Jung's theory of liminal space:** Along with Freud and Adler, Carl Jung was a founding father of psychoanalysis and one of his most significant concepts was liminal space which refers to our developmental efforts to transcend our station in life and get to the next level. Liminal space is like a doorway, and it is filled with anxiety, pressure, challenges, and confusion. Liminal space is a useful concept for the sport psychologist because it highlights the challenging transitions from high school ball to college and then from college to the pros. The case of the Olympic sprinter who became frozen in the blocks during the Olympic Trials will be used to demonstrate the challenges of liminal space and explains why many athletes often fail to transition through liminal space into the next stage in their sport.

**Anna Freud's theory of defenses:** Anna Freud wrote about how the ego manages internal pressures through defenses. I will discuss how athletes use a variety of defenses including repression, denial, acting out, regression, suppression, somatization, intellectualization, displacement, sublimation, and humor to cope with internal and external pressures. The cognitive behavioral approach does not show any awareness of how varied defenses can be and seem to suggest that intellectualization and suppression are the only two defenses that athletes need. This seriously underestimates the variety of defenses regularly used by athletes to cope with their stress and competitive anxiety. Successful athletes need several very strong and well-established defenses to enable them to withstand the intense pressure they face. Many younger athletes have poor and primitive defenses. I would suggest that the bulk of the mental skills training taking place today are haphazard atheoretical attempts to create defenses for the athletes with no regard for what the athlete is currently using nor which newer defenses need to be learned. We will explore both effective and ineffective defenses seen in athletes and discuss how to replace weak immature defenses with stronger more mature ones.

**Heinz Kohut's theory of narcissism:** Heinz Kohut led the way to a deeper understanding of narcissism. Traits of narcissism are seen in many of today's entitled professional athletes. Kohut's theory of self-psychology focused on the self as opposed to Freudian drive states (Kohut, 1977), and he discussed how a poorly developed sense of self produced a brittle shell of arrogance, grandiosity and pseudo-independence and explained how the desperate need for applause drives performers and athletes. There remains much controversy about how narcissism develops and what to do about it but Robert Millman, former Medical Director of Major League Baseball made a crucial addition by discussing late-onset narcissism or "Acquired Situational Narcissism" after he began noticing a pattern in his celebrity athlete patients (Lowin, Ruiz, Millman, and Langrod, 2006). He felt that when fame occurs during teen years this can produce a distorted sense of entitlement, poor decision making, drug use, unstable relationships and divorce. This form of Late Onset Narcissism is maintained by the fans, media attention, the entourage and groupies that surround the star. Many star athletes are suffering with Acquired Situational Narcissism, and I will show how this leads to drug use, unstable relationships and eventual loneliness, chaos, and despair. The issue of resistance by the narcissist is rarely discussed in the sport psychology literature yet is one of the most obvious problems sport psychologists face. Kohut's theory of the treatment of narcissism lends itself to work with athletes who suffer with these characterological traits. His strategies along with Millman's serve as invaluable guides when working with narcissistic athletes and this will be discussed in the chapter on chipping yips.

**Margaret Mahler's theory of separation/individuation:** Margaret Mahler's theory of separation/individuation defined how children learn to separate and become independent (Mahler, 1969). We will explore how winning is sometimes feared by athletes because it symbolizes a separation from early childhood bonds with family. This is what some call the fear of success and explains how lapses in focus, choking or getting weak when finishing off a tournament is due to an unconscious separation anxiety. In these cases, the therapist needs to function as a transitional object as the athlete approaches victory. Margaret Mahler's ideas on separation and individuation serve as useful tools in the effort to get an athlete to reach their full potential and to overcome patterns of self-defeat. A case study of a professional tennis player who choked during the finals will be used to demonstrate how winning symbolized a separation from his schizophrenic mother which produced unconscious guilt in him.

**Melanie Klein's theory of envy:** Klein developed a theory describing the child's natural destructive nature and how envious they were of what others possessed. Klein's writings influenced the development of the British Object Relations School, and her theory helps to explain the feelings of envy and jealousy often manifested on teams. It is always a shock to me when I am hired by professional teams and observe how much envy, hatred and backstabbing occurs in the locker room. This is one of professional sports dirty little secrets. Phil Jackson created the Chicago Bulls basketball dynasty by instinctively knowing how to manage the extreme envy elicited in the team upon the arrival of Michael Jordan. Envy and jealousy are frequently mismanaged, and I will describe how a young rookie star in the NBA was destroyed by the jealousy of a super star teammate who resented the fact that the young star was getting more press. Melanie Klein's work is well suited to help us treat teams plagued with envy, a dynamic that has destroyed many a sports franchise. Standard sport psychology has little to say on this matter, apparently denying these toxic emotions.

**Ronald Fairbairn's theory of the Internal Saboteur:** Contrary to Freud, Fairbairn's theory stated that the child is not pleasure seeking but rather love seeking and suggested that when a child is chronically ignored or mistreated, they turn away from the hope for love and instead create an unconscious world. Part of this inner world contains the Internal Saboteur, a dissociated organized state triggered when the athlete approaches success. The Internal Saboteur insists that a perpetual state of misery remain. I will describe how the application of Fairbairn's theory of the Internal Saboteur helped a famous athlete I treated to finally resolve a pattern of self-defeat that cost him tens of millions in endorsement dollars and purses.

**Wilfred Bion's theory of regression in groups:** Bion worked mostly with groups in a hospital setting and he produced a potent and insightful theory of group functioning which is now used by the A. K. Rice Institute in its work with governments and corporations throughout the world. To date, no one has used his group theory to analyze or treat sports franchises. Bion suggested that when becoming part of a group, people will often regress into non-productive, childlike attitudes which he called Basic Assumptions. His three Basic Assumptions included Dependency, Fight/Flight, and Pairing. The Dependency Assumption is seen when a group becomes passive, expecting one member to do all the work. You see this when a team has a super star which prompts the rest to lay back and rest. This is referred to as social loafing and though behavioral therapists seem to be aware of this issue, they do not reference a coherent theory to explain it. The Fight/Flight Assumption is when the group would fight amongst themselves rather than working to fight their opponents. The film "Any Given Sunday" starring Jamie Foxx and Al Pacino exemplified the Fight /Flight Assumption very well. The endless fighting seen on teams is a constant headache for coaches and GM's. The third Basic Assumption was called Pairing which was seen when a group becomes passive and hopes that two members would take over the job of creativity. We will review a few cases of teams that regressed into these basic assumptions and how this theory can help coaches in their efforts to manage group regression.

**Christopher Bollas' theory of the transformational object:** Christopher Bollas is a leading figure in the British School of Object Relations and his concept of the transformational object clarifies athletes' motives to win. He explains that patients search for transformational objects such as trophies or awards in the hope that they will be transformed by them like the search for the magical cure offered by the holy grail. Bollas believes that adults compulsively seek experiences like love, trophies, travel, or aesthetic moments in order to transform their damaged self into a better one. The chapter on an acute depression in an athlete who was given Rookie of the Year Award in baseball will demonstrate the childlike wishes and inevitable disappointments contained in these transformational objects.

The psychoanalytic theories mentioned above have rarely been used to understand or to treat athletes, their anxiety, mood problems or inclinations to self-defeat and in the next chapter we will explore the basic techniques used by psychoanalysts.

## References

Adler, A. (1964) *Individual Psychology of Alfred Adler.* HarperCollins Publishers.

Bion, W. (1975) Experiences in Groups. In *Group Relations Reader 1*, Eds, A. Colman and H. Bexton. A. K. Rice Institute.

Bollas, C. (1987) *The Shadow of the Object. Psychoanalysis of the Unthought Known.* Columbia University Press.

Fairbairn, R. (1952) *Psychoanalytic Studies of the Personality.* Tavistock/Routledge.

Freud, S. (1923/1961) *The Ego and the Id, The Standard Edition of the Complete Psychological Works of Sigmund Freud*, Vol. 19. Translated and edited by L. Strachey. Hogarth Press, pp. 1–66.

Freud, A. (1937) *The Ego and the Mechanisms of Defense.* International University Press.

Jung, C. (1956) Symbols of Transformation (*Collected Works of C.G. Jung*, Vol. 5). Princeton University Press.

Klein, M. (1969) *Envy, Gratitude and Other Works.* Tavistock Press.

Kohut, H. (1977) *The Restoration of the Self.* The International Universities Press.

Lowinsan, J, Ruiz, P. Millman, R., and Longrad, J. (Eds) (2006) *Substance Abuse: A Comprehensive Textbook* (4th Ed.). Lippincott Williams and Wilkins.

Mahler, M. (1969)*On Human Symbiosis and the Vicissitudes of Individuation*, Vol. 1. Hogarth Press.

Suarez-Orozco, M. (1999) A Psychoanalytic Study of Argentine Soccer. In *Psychoanalysis and Culture at the Millennium*, Eds, N. Ginsburg and R. Ginsburg. Yale University Press, pp. 64–95.

# 3 Psychoanalytic Techniques Used with Athletes

Over the past 120 years, psychoanalysts have developed a series of techniques necessary to effectuate a cure. These include the working alliance, the therapeutic framework, the rule of free association, dream analysis, the interpretation of parapraxis or errors in speech or action (i.e., Freudian slips), the use of interpretation, confronting resistance, and the interpretation of transference and counter transference. We will discuss each of these techniques and how psychoanalysis encourages the free expression of thoughts and emotions to interpret these thoughts based upon the patient's history and psychodynamics.

**The working alliance:** In psychoanalysis, the working alliance consists of the friendly feeling established between therapist and the athlete through empathy, positive regard, and a non-judgmental attitude. This approach usually comes naturally to psychotherapists. As a comfortable relationship is formed, symptoms and problem traits are discussed. The analyst creates a psychodynamic formulation which connects the symptoms to the athlete's past. The working alliance established by the psychoanalyst does not differ markedly from the way a typical sport psychologist would work but the orientation is far different. In cognitive/behavioral therapy, there is a belief that the work will be short term and thus a working alliance is not so crucial. But in long term psychodynamic psychotherapy, the analyst expects resistance to emerge anywhere between five to ten sessions and this resistance can be handled more readily if a solid working alliance is first formed. In a typical course of therapy, the emergence of resistance is expressed with missed appointments and a sudden and premature desire to terminate. Cognitive/behavioral therapy circumvents the issue of resistance by beating the athlete to the punch with the suggestion that brief five to ten sessions short term therapy are sufficient in establishing a cure.

**Establishing the framework:** The first rule in psychoanalysis is to establish the therapeutic framework, and it is one of the hardest rules to follow. Elite and professional athletes are constantly on the move, pulled in a variety of directions and pressed for time, so establishing a consistent framework of weekly appointment times in a private setting is problematic. The analyst's ability to establish and maintain a regular appointment time

DOI: 10.4324/9781003272465-3

allows the athlete to feel he or she is in the presence of a professional which ensures respect and if this is maintained the athlete develops trust in the holding power of the analyst, relaxes his guard, and divulges more. Establishing the framework means that the analyst has a private office that is sound proofed and with separate entrance and exits so that the athlete's confidentiality is guarded. This is crucially important when working with well-known athletes. My father was friends with Joe DiMaggio at the height of his fame and I recall him saying that DiMaggio could not make a regular appointment with his dentist. It always had to be after hours to avoid other patients in the waiting room asking for autographs. Working with star athletes requires that the analyst maintain and guard their privacy carefully. When a predictable, safe, and private framework is established, the athlete will start to divulge their hidden thoughts and feelings. And when a regular time slot is established, it becomes possible to assess the meaning of missed sessions as a part of resistance and acting out. Acting out through missing appointments is usually an attempt to avoid painful affects, or it is an attempt to project feelings of loss or helplessness into the analyst.

**The rule of free association**: Free association is the fundamental rule of psychoanalysis and encourages the patient to say whatever comes into their heads, even if they think it unimportant, irrelevant, nonessential, or embarrassing (Breuer and Freud, 1895). This practice is based upon the belief that each patient has the power to approach their own unconscious indirectly if allowed to talk in an uninterrupted fashion. This technique is the opposite of the standard cognitive behavioral approach, which encourages suppression of thoughts and feelings rather than expressing them.

Prior to the discovery of this method, Freud used methods like cognitive behaviorists by cajoling, encouraging, instructing, directing, insisting, educating, and hypnotizing the patients into giving up their anxious symptoms (Freud, 1899). He eventually learned that insistent pushing towards the cure served only to delay the work and produced nothing more than resistance and premature terminations. He finally came upon the method of free association whereby the patient was to relax into a free-flowing conversation and say whatever comes to mind. The analyst's job was to attend to the patient's associations without guidance or interruption and by so doing attune his unconscious to the patient's unconscious.

To listen attentively and without interrupting the patient prematurely is difficult but if the therapist allows the patient to free associate, the stream of consciousness gives way to what we call unconscious derivatives which are underlying concerns that are pressing into consciousness (Langs, 1973). The task of the therapist is to listen and retain the themes that the patient explores step by step. By the end of the session, the therapist's task is to synthesize these interconnected themes in the broadest way possible and by so doing reveal the underlying issue that is being expressed. This is a difficult task and requires good short and middle term memory, relaxed focus, and patience, and this is a skill that takes years to develop.

When athletes are allowed to free associate, and not be judged, they become freer, more spontaneous, and more able to take risks on the playing field.

Screen memories will emerge during free association and are the seemingly bland memories from childhood but will often contain crucial material that reveals early fixations and trauma. An example of a screen memory was seen in a patient of mine who was an elite swimmer suffering with exhaustion and injuries. One of his childhood memories was climbing on top of monkey bars in the playground when he was eight years old and throwing all his cherished baseball cards into the air for all the other kids in the playground to have. This benign memory was eventually seen to be a screen memory of his hopeless and helpless efforts to keep his fragmented family from falling apart. Uncovering this screen memory was the first key in explaining his compulsive overwork, his exhaustion, and his injuries.

Free association may have been the first instrument for the scientific exploration of the human mind and its use helps them to be more creative, less anxious, less defensive, more open, more free, more confident, and a more interesting person overall.

**The use of interpretations:** Interpretation is the analyst's efforts to explain the athlete's symptoms with their forgotten past. Interpretation connects the 'here and now' to the 'then and there.' Sport psychology has tried to deny the past and provides mental tools to enhance performance in the here and now. Depth sport psychology endeavors to teach the patient to seek understanding of the connection between current woes and past problems and when that occurs, they will be less conflicted, more self-aware, and then more able to use suppressive tools effectively.

As the athlete free associates, the analyst keeps track of emerging themes and can make interpretations. The rule is to interpret what is most recent in the patient's past and work backwards from there. If they suffered a big loss last week, that is discussed prior to what happen last year. Interpretations must be correct, timed properly and not rushed or they will fall flat and create more resistance. Freud called this "Wild Analysis" (Freud, 1910).

Later in the book I will discuss the free associations of a major league pitcher who had problems with control based upon overthrowing. His free associations revealed that overthrowing was triggered by a compulsion to keep pushing and not acknowledge success based upon his father's attitude and insecurity. The interpretation was that he was identifying with his anxious father and had incorporated this anxious self-doubting overzealous attitude on the mound. This interpretation had an immediate and long-lasting impact as he learned to create his own more mature strategies for success.

**Dream analysis:** Freud called dreams "the royal road to the unconscious" and felt that by analyzing a patient's dream you could uncover their most deep-rooted conflicts. Psychoanalytic dream analysis is an elaborate process, taking one or two sessions per dream as you uncover the meaning of the symbols expressed in the dream. Dreams use the mechanisms of condensation, displacement, visualization, and symbolism. Condensation means one dream symbol can represent many hidden ideas. Visualization means that thoughts are often displaced into a visual image in dreams. An example of a dream reported by John Updike the author/golf enthusiast goes like this. He is out with his usual foursome and has his ball teed up and ready to swing. But as he looks down the fairway the trees get more numerous, the fairway tighter and his driver becomes rubbery rather than stiff. He looks down at his ball and it transforms itself from round to cylindrical and is a pill box now. He swings away and proceeds down the fairway in a jaunty fashion. One does not have to be Sigmund Freud to understand some of the more obvious concerns expressed therein including fear of competition, fear of failure, and feeling powerless with a flaccid penis. In the chapter on athletes and their dreams I will share some dreams that we analyzed and what we discovered of their meaning. Almost invariably, the athlete will feel that when their dreams are analyzed correctly the insights are surprising and helpful.

**Freudian slips, parapraxis, accidents, and mistakes:** Freudian slips or parapraxis are errors in speech, memory or physical action that occur, owing to an unconscious wish or conflict. Parapraxis includes slips of the tongue, misreading's, mishearing's, mistyping's, temporary forgetting, mis-placing, or losing objects. For athletes, parapraxis on the playing field is seen in dropped passes, yips or missed tee times and their analysis can be extremely revealing. I have been witness to many of these mysterious 'mistakes,' perhaps the most egregious was in 1999, when golfer Bruce Fleisher, on the Champions Tour, nearly lost the Lightpath Long Island Classic thanks to two parapraxis. He almost missed his tee time on Saturday when he misread his time. On the next day, with a four-shot lead on the 18th green, he moved his ball mark to accommodate another player. He failed to return his ball to the proper spot and was about to sign his score card which would have resulted in disqualification if not for a fan shouting that he did not move his ball mark back. This only cost him two shots rather than a DQ. In this case the two parapraxis or Freudian slips was explained by realizing that Bruce's two dear friends had passed away the week before and he was experiencing survivor guilt and a need for punishment. We will discuss the common occurrence of parapraxis or "Freudian slips" in sports during our case studies later in the book.

**Confronting resistance:** Handling of resistance is one of the cornerstones of psychoanalysis, yet standard sport psychology texts make no mention of this problem. Resistance is defined as all the forces which oppose the process of the treatment. The force of resistance opposes insight and change. Resistance is great in athletes who feel stigmatized by seeking help. Resistance is expressed through silence, affectless dialogue, discussing trivia, avoidance of topics, lateness, missed appointments or failure to pay, yawning, acting out, frequent cheerfulness, and sudden terminations. Resistance is seen when athletes are confronted with difficult transitions from high school to college or college to pros. Often you see unconscious cognitive dissonance or conflict between their view of themselves and their view of the demands they are about to face. Examples resistance will be discussed in many chapters throughout the book.

**Transference/counter transference**: Freud has stated that the only cure is the transference cure. Transference is all the distorted feelings and perceptions in a patient that are caused by early childhood experiences with parents or siblings. As an example, if a patient had a parent or older sibling that was hostile, threatening, or jealous, the athlete will see their opponent as threatening and hostile as well and will be overly anxious. They are transferring fear of a hostile parent onto an opponent, and this spells defeat. This process was first explained by Freud in his essay "Repeating, Remembering and Working Through." And when these transferential issues are not resolved, the athlete remains trapped and destined to repeat the losses endlessly. Transference in the therapy is seen when the patient sees the therapist as acting like a parent or sibling. When these distortions are sensed by the analyst this is called counter transference and the distortions can be studied and worked through. This is often a very delicate and difficult process to manage but very helpful and it will lead to genuine and healing dialogue. We will touch on a few examples of transference interpretations in our case studies.

Counter transference are the feelings experienced by the therapist when working with the athlete. Strong counter transference is often felt when working with world famous athletes and this counter transference can prompt one to be overly flexible regarding missed appointments. It is astounding to me that there is so little mention of this dynamic in any of the cognitive behavioral texts, yet it is invariably felt and must be handled. An example of breaking the framework, owing to counter transference by the therapist was seen in the world of entertainment. Marilyn Monroe, who was at that time the most famous entertainer on earth, enlisted the help of Dr. Ralph Greenson, a renowned psychotherapist who lived in Los Angeles and had written one of the key textbooks in psychoanalysis. Greenson agreed to treat Ms. Monroe, but he became so mesmerized by the combination of her beauty, fragility, and sexual power that eventually he invited her to move into his house and continued to treat her like a family member. The world knows the outcome of that failed analysis. Ms. Monroe eventually committed suicide. This is a good example of why the framework is crucial and how the counter transference produced when treating super stars can easily weaken and destroy any chance for a cure. I will discuss my counter transference when treating a super star.

These are the essential techniques that are used by psychoanalysts when working with patients and these are the techniques I use with athletes. Each chapter will demonstrate one technique, and a sidebar will detail the method used.

## References

Breuer, J. and Freud, S. (1895/1955) Studies in Hysteria. In *The Standard Edition of the Complete Psychological Works of Sigmund Freud*, Vol. 11, Ed. J. Strachey. Hogarth Press.

Freud, S. (1899) Introductory lectures on Psychoanalysis. In *The Standard Edition of the Complete Works of Sigmund Freud*, Vol. 11, Ed. J. Strachey. Hogarth Press, p. 236.

Freud. S. (1910) "Wild" Psycho-analysis. In A. Phillips, Ed. *Sigmund Freud: Wild Analysis*. Penguin, p. 1–10.

Langs, R. (1973) *The Technique of Psychoanalytic Psychotherapy*, Vol. 1. Jason Aronson.

# 4 The Athletes' Motivation Viewed as a Repetition Compulsion

This 28-year-old golfer came to me with complaints of anxiety and putting yips while playing golf and that he became overly distracted and annoyed with his opponents. His history revealed that he was small for his age and the youngest in his class throughout schooling. He had excelled in every sport he played and enjoyed football most of all, but his talent meant he was always playing with older boys who decided he was an easy target for abuse and bullied him relentlessly. The football culture is aggressive, and it produced enough anxiety in the patient that he was forced to transfer schools but damage to his self-esteem was already entrenched within him. He eventually attended an Ivy League college and grew into a man of high intellectual ability, social grace, was tall in stature and good looking, assets that afforded him almost limitless opportunities were he to pursue and business career. Instead, he decided to embark on a dubious quest to become a professional golfer. By the age of 25, after three years of sacrifice, which included travel, expensive lessons from the world's best swing instructors, and personal trainers, he was getting nowhere, suffered anxiety during every round and he contacted me in the hope that he might learn how to manage his anxieties more effectively on the golf course.

He told me of how distracted and anxious he felt when he played against anyone, no matter how inferior they were in talent. We began to connect this anxiety with the traumatic bullying he had experienced in his youth and eventually we discussed how his compulsive drive to win on the playing field was a counter phobic repetition compulsion or a need to face down the bullies he had endured as a young teen. Winning in golf would be his revenge.

**On Repetition Compulsions:** Freud was the first to suggest that when childhood traumas are repressed and unresolved, we seek out situations later in life that resemble the initial traumas to master them. This theory was presented in his paper "Repeating, Remembering and Working Through" (Freud, 1911). Freud felt people were like the Greek King Sisyphus who was condemned to eternally push a huge boulder up a hill only to have it roll down each time it neared the top. As you will see shortly, the repetition

DOI: 10.4324/9781003272465-4

compulsion is exactly what operant conditioners call negative reinforcement or when something unpleasant is taken away after a behavior is performed. But with the repetition compulsion the self-defeating behavior continues on ad infinitum since there is no insight gained.

Similar to Freud's concept, Fenichel (1939) suggested that sport is a counter-phobic endeavor, and the essential joy of sport is the opportunity to recreate earlier childhood traumatic situations so that one can face them down and triumph. Helene Deutsch (1999) also wrote that the repetition compulsion was a way the athlete managed earlier trauma. As an example, if a baseball batter has a deep-rooted fear of an abusive father, then every time he faces a pitcher, he symbolically faces his father, and a hit is a triumph over this trauma.

The repetition compulsion also applies to the professional athlete. After Tiger Woods first $500 million, he surely was no longer in need of cash, yet he preserved much like Sisyphus, endlessly pushing that boulder up the mountain. Most Olympic athletes willingly give ten years of their life for a chance to win a gold medal with virtually no way to receive adequate monetary compensation. And the typical childhood of a future professional athlete reveals a compulsive devotion to their sport. Research shows that during the early years, the future professional practices far more than the average youngster, often to the point of fatigue, exhaustion, personality change and injury (Faigenbaum, 2009). So, a crucial question is what compels people to sacrifice their body, their time, and their childhood to play a game?

What possessed my patient to sacrifice so many years in a punishing endeavor was an underlying motivation to face his childhood bullies and triumph over them. Efforts at mastering childhood traumas through sports accounts for the compulsive hold that sports have on many athletes. This compulsion sometimes can result in fame, money, and success, but it can also lead to exhaustion and a reluctance to retire. Athletes need help to see the source of their motives which often can lead to undo anxiety, burnout, and overuse injuries. Resolving neurotic issues in no way undermines the athlete's desire to win but instead helps to free them of their fears, their compulsions and allows them ways to find calm while under pressure and give them permission to obtain the rest which is a part of a successful sports career.

Over a two-year period, this athlete came to the realization that his revenge motivation was self-destructive to himself, and he slowly reoriented himself towards a career in finance and went on to use this golf game as an essential and helpful networking tool in his business life. All's well that ends well. We can see how the severe bullying in his youth, produced a repetition compulsion to address this trauma through sports and that this kind of compulsive motive did not serve him well. Insight into this past dynamic allowed him to make a reasonable decision and to turn his energies to more productive and rewarding pursuits.

## References

Deutsch, H. (1999) A Contribution to the Psychology of Sport. In *The Therapeutic Process, the Self and Female Psychology*. Routledge.

Faigenbaum, A. (2009) Overtraining in Young Athletes. *Health and Fitness Journal*, 13(4): 8–13.

Fenichel, O. (1939) *The Counter-Phobic Attitude, The International Journal of Psychoanalysis*, Vol. 20: 263.

Freud, S. (1911–1913) *The Standard Edition of the Complete Psychological Works of Sigmund Freud*, Vol. XII.

# Part I

# Case Studies of Anxiety in Sports

# 5 The Cause and Cure of a Golfer's Chipping Yips

Anxiety is expressed in a variety of ways including tension, worry, overthinking, chest pain, weakness, butterflies in the stomach, nausea, vomiting, muscle spasms, lightheadedness, dizziness, muscle pain, cold clammy hands or feet, a choking feeling, or a sense of impending doom. One or more of these symptoms can wreak havoc on athletic performance and in the following section, we will discuss the underlying reasons why the athlete experiences anxiety and how the psychoanalyst helps them to understand and resolve this frequent issue.

The yips come suddenly and leave reluctantly. They are an expression of extreme anxiety and are a sign that a player is no longer able to manage the tension they are experiencing. This kind of collapse is often experienced by young prodigies who have achieved world ranking and early fame but whose defenses are not yet equipped to manage this kind of pressure. By age 14, this young golfer was labeled her sport's next super star and was ranked # 1 junior in the world. She was constantly being interviewed, given special invites to play in LPGA events and free memberships at a prestigious country club. She was riding high on the wave of celebrity when the attention, adulation and pressure suddenly coalesced into the chipping yips. At 14, she first experienced the yips when playing in an LPGA event under a special invite and she described it as a numbing of her hands and arms. She suffered with the yips throughout her teens and early 20's. Her talent allowed her to manage her anxiety to some degree but by her mid-twenties she was languishing on one of the mini tours in Asia, the minor leagues of golf.

By the time she contacted me, she had already seen a few of the game's most prominent sport psychologists and been given the standard suppressive behavioral techniques including visualization, relaxation tips, goal setting, and positive self-talk to control her anxieties. These treatments had no discernible impact on her yips. She then turned to drug use and self-medication by using a combination of marijuana, beta blockers, Valium, and antidepressants when faced with tournament stress. These drugs did help with her anxiety but the side effects for a professional golfer are devastating in a game requiring delicate feel and acute focus. There is no drug in

DOI: 10.4324/9781003272465-6

existence outside of caffeine, which has shown to improve athletic performance (Wadler and Hainline, 1989). The medication side effects impacted her scoring negatively. I had met her while on a book tour in South Korea when she was still a youngster in a golf academy in Seoul. Her coach told me then that she was destined to be a super star and ten years later, when she came across one of my psychoanalytic articles on the yips, she gave me a call.

Her history revealed that at age 12 she was the highest ranked young golfer in Asia, by 14 she was world #1 and was labeled the next Tiger Woods for women. She played well and freely, had a phenomenal short game, and was trained by a teaching pro in Asia. Her good looks, extraordinary talent, precocity, and wins on the national junior circuit led to special invitations to play in LPGA events where she was exposed to more media attention, television appearances and headlines in papers who described her as "The Golden Girl." She was given a modeling contract given her good looks, and finally she had such extraordinary talent that she was given an invite into a men's PGA event in Hawaii. Finally, during one of her rounds in a men's event while still 14 years old, she developed a numbing feeling in her arms and her chipping yips began and she began to crack.

Initially we did spend time exploring suppressive techniques but once again these had no impact. Her yips were an accumulation of traumatic experiences based upon the jealousy of peers and overwhelming expectations placed on her young shoulders. She realized at this point in her career that if she did not address these pervasive deeper issues, her career was finished.

Her lifestyle before and after fame was a tale of two cities. Before fame, she was a normal hard-working kid from a blue-collar family in Seoul, South Korea, who had a very special talent and enjoyed the game of golf. Her coach was also a blue-collar guy with a hardnosed approach who supported her well. But as she began to receive national attention from the press and the LPGA, her attitude began to change, and she became distracted by fame. She was given special privileges at country clubs, approached by world famous swing coaches and gradually a change in her personality occurred. She began to work less hard, as if she had already arrived and was now on easy street. She lost focus on the game itself and instead spent time grooming her image and social persona, like the way tennis star Naomi Osaka described her experience growing up in the limelight. As her chipping yips worsened, her work effort diminished, and grandiosity became intermingled with mounting stress and growing despair. Owing to her talent, reputation, and record, she was given a full college scholarship despite her chipping yips. Fame grew, her work ethic lessened, and she developed an excessive interest in appearance. This had all the signs of late onset narcissism.

**Robert B. Millman on Acquired Situational Narcissism:** Dr. Millman, the former Medical Director of Major League Baseball, worked with a variety of sports celebrities, and he was the first to describe Acquired Situational Narcissism or Late-Onset Narcissism (Lowinsan, Ruiz, Millman, and Langrod, 2006). This character trait develops during teenage years and is seen in those who acquire fame at a young age and adopt the traits of entitlement, poor decision making, drug use, damage to any stable relationships, and who are prone to a variety of illegal or immoral behaviors based upon their feelings of omnipotence. No apparent narcissism exists prior to this but the disorder emerges and is enabled by the media, fans and their entourage of assistants, agents, publicists, lawyers, and groupies who tolerate, condone, or applaud their selfish behavior.

By the age of 15 she already had an agent who complicated things even more by suggesting she medicate her anxiety with beta blockers, valium and antidepressants. At this point the athlete had all the traits of Acquired Situational Narcissism including entitlement, laziness, drug use, excessive interest in appearance, poor decision making, behaviors that bordered on illegal, and she was being enabled by agents, fans and financial supporters who wanted to be associated with a rising star.

This case demonstrates how the pressure of great expectations and fame established a personality disorder in this patient and how problematic it was for her to escape it. Winnicott wrote that a false self is created at the hands of an exploitative parent (Winnicott, 1971), but in this case fame and an entourage play the role of an exploiting parent and create this false self in the athlete. This complicated case required a working through of her personality disorder, the resolving of her drug dependence and working through of the traumatic shame experienced when she yipped. Furthermore, the yips acted as a defense, preventing her from winning and keeping her away from the big-league pressure, that she claimed to want. As she entered therapy, she was developmentally fixated at age 14, confused, terrified, helpless, and overwhelmed.

Approaching this player with simplistic positive psychology self-talk borders on the absurd yet that is what she was handed for the past ten years. Elite athletes are under constant pressure and must manage fame, adoration, expectation, and loss of privacy. This experience will often change an athlete's personality. The work of helping them is far from simple, easy, or quick. The work must first establish a dynamic picture of what has happened to them. In many ways this athlete was still a 14-year-old girl trapped in a body of a 24-year-old. The methodology used with an athlete who remains fixated at the age of her initial shattering is to help her to share, remember and to understand what occurred to her all through her career so that she can grow beyond it into a more mature and stronger person, with better defenses which enable her to withstand the distractions of pressure and fame. I used Kohut's model of treatment for narcissism (Kohut, 1977) and endeavored to remain attuned to her past traumas, shame, and losses, as well as her achievements and talent. Attunement is always difficult especially when there is acting out with missed appointments etc. As Kohut suggested, attunement slowly helps the patient to find their true self, their self-worth, and finally the ability to bounce back from mistakes on the course. This is a long process of repairing of the ego and to suggest that all one needs is some positive self-talk is doing a disservice to the athlete and to the field itself.

## References

Kohut, H. (1977) *The Restoration of the Self.* International Universities Press.

Lowinsan, J., Ruiz, P., Millman, and R. Langrod, J. (Eds) (2006) *Substance Abuse: A Comprehensive Textbook* (4th Ed.). Lippincott Williams and Wilkins.

Wadler, G. and Hainline, B. (1989)*Drugs and the Athlete.* F.A. Davis Company.

Winnicott, D. (1971) *Playing and Reality*. Penguin Books.

# 6 Mediocrity and the Fear of Success

This is the case of a professional golfer who suffered athletic disappointments and shame in college which instilled fear of failures later in life. He unconsciously developed a defense of playing mediocre golf which prevented him from entering this state of helpless anxiety when in the lead. I have often been told by athletes "Well if I don't really try, I won't feel so bad if I lose" and this is what we mean by 'fear of success.' The threat of losing where athletes are equally matched will often induce great fear and result in an unconscious defense and avoidance of this experience. The athlete will demote him or herself, and embrace a more mediocre functioning to avoid the feeling of anxiety and loss. Unresolved losses often present as a lack of focus when the player gets close to winning. The underlying cause of poor focus and mediocre effort will often derive from an intolerable loss that may have occurred years ago that the athlete is afraid to re-experience. The athlete unconsciously develops an avoidance of excellence, and this defense protects them from ever entering situations that might force them to experience the loss again. Each time they see victory come into view, they back off and become weak, passive, negative, filled with despair, and lose focus. I believe this is an exceptionally common problem in sports.

This patient was expected to become a high-level tour professional but instead wound up struggling to compete in local amateur events despite obvious talent. He could never escape from the primary loss. As a youngster, this golfer rose to the highest level in America. He won AJGA events and beat most of the biggest names in amateur golf. This led to a full scholarship to college where he played next to the likes of Jordan Spieth and Justin Thomas. But his dream of glory was quickly destroyed when he faced college competition that was equal to him if not better. He was no longer the big man on campus and this loss of status induced a crisis of identity, helpless anxiety, and self-doubt. His college coach began to make swing change suggestions which only worsened matters and his entire college experience was disastrous. He lost his swing, and his scholarship and sat back and watched as his teammates grew into world famous stars and he eventually slouched his way home in defeat. He took up a job in his family business and thereafter he entered amateur events on a local level.

DOI: 10.4324/9781003272465-7

In the past, prior to college, he had no trouble winning tournaments. But in college his swing became mechanical, tentative, and weak. He felt shame, despair, anxiety, and confusion. He became a mediocre player, habitually playing well below potential, and seemed to be trapped there. He took to reading all the current self-help sport psychology books but with no real gains. He kept practicing, took lessons, and played in events but whenever he came close to victory, he lost form and backed away. In horse racing jargon, this is called 'spitting the bit.'

**Fear of Success:** Bibring (1953) suggested that weakness, apathy, depression and self-preoccupation are often used as a defense to avoid the helplessness endured during competition especially when the athlete is trying to close in on a win. He felt that threats to self-esteem may feel intolerable and must be defended against by an inhibition of function. I believe this dynamic is common in sports and explains why so many athletes back away from victory as they approach it. Furthermore, this dynamic has never been discussed in the literature and the only player I recall ever talking about the fear of success was Jack Nicklaus, who was aware that most of his competitors would back off at the end.

In this case, our sessions focused on the unbearable disappointment and loss that occurred in those four college years and the helplessness and disappointment he experienced.

All athletes lose on occasion and the question is how they manage these losses. In this case, unbearable loss was managed by developing a defense which avoided this kind of loss ever again. He became avoidant of victory, feared it and developed mediocrity as the answer, similar to Salieri in the film "Amadeus" as he proudly announced to the other patients in the insane asylum that he was indeed "The Prince of Mediocrity."

In post-traumatic stress cases, patients will avoid going near the place where the initial trauma occurred. For this traumatized golfer, the place he feared most of all was reentering the heat of battle. The athlete unconsciously set his goals at a lower level thereby avoiding the possibility of unbearable loss. This is the defense of mediocrity. The benefit of this strategy is that it protects them from feeling helplessness and shame ever again, but at a cost since they live out a mediocre athletic career, fail to reach full potential, and at times resort to alcohol or marijuana for solace.

In depth sport psychology we discussed current performance failures, trace them back to those fixated moments of despair in the past and explore the helplessness and hopelessness that is still within. As we begin to identify when this defense emerged, the golfer began to develop more courage to face risks once again. When insight like this is worked through over time the athlete feels repaired, gets stronger and braver, and begins to allow themselves to experience risk and to embrace their power, talent, drive, ambition, and focus. Pride grows, performance becomes more natural and fluid, and finally victory is once again obtained. This is what occurred with this golfer as we worked on new defenses to replace his avoidance strategy. We discussed identification with the aggressor as I taught him how to act like an alpha male, with a swaggering body language, cool aggressive attitude and overall cockiness. In addition, they learn to give themselves comfort and solace when they fail.

The process unfolds gradually and often the athlete can only verbalize that he or she is playing better and feels more self-forgiving. This case demonstrates the complicated process of insight, visitation of the past, ego repair, loss resolution and the building of new defenses. This amounts to far more than "just do it' slogans but instead looks back at the initial traumas that are still exerting influence in strange ways.

## References

Bibring, E. The Mechanism of Depression. In *Affective Disorders*, Ed. P. Greenacre. International Universities Press, pp. 13–48.

Freud, S. 1957. Some character types met with in psycho-analytic work. In J. Strachey (Ed. & Trans.), *Standard Edition of the Complete Psychological Work of Sigmund Freud*, Vol.14,. Hogarth Press (original work published 1916), pp. 309–333.

# 7 Serving Yips in Tennis

People live two lives simultaneously. They live their current life and their past life at the same time. Unconscious childhood anxiety, shame, sadness, or anger shadows many athletes throughout their career. When the past has an undue influence on the present, we call this a neurosis and there is not an adult alive today that does not suffer from some form of neurotic influence. We live in the present but are chased and often caught by our past.

This is the case of an amateur tennis player stuck in the world of his anxious tormented middle school years. He came to me complaining of the yips while serving which produced an embarrassing inability to get his serves over the net. This is a widespread problem seen in tennis players. Curiously, he did not suffer when serving in singles events but only when partnering with another player in doubles matches.

He had been a college tennis player and upon graduation began his career as an attorney while continuing to play high level amateur tennis. Over the years he began to experience yips when he was partnered with someone. He had a series of coaches who tried to help him manage his yips with the standard psychological tools for anxiety suppression including self-talk, deep breathing, and forms of visualization, but no improvement was seen.

After an intake and history taking, I explained the process of psychoanalytic therapy and how to free associate.

> Free association is the backbone of analytic treatment, and is a way to enter and explore the unconscious. The patient is told to begin talking about whatever comes to mind without filtering in any way. This can be quite problematic because of shame, guilt, lack of trust or embarrassment on the part of the athlete. But as trust and ego strength develop and if a good alliance has been established, free association unfolds and real insight into the unconscious can occur. In addition, the practice of free associating generalizes into more spontaneity outside the office both in social interactions as well as on the playing field. To date, this issue has received no attention in the literature and is a splendid dissertation area.

DOI: 10.4324/9781003272465-8

This patient had good intelligence, good verbal skills and enough trust to free associate easily. Within a few sessions he was talking at length about his teenage experiences and the high-pressured social life of the private high school he attended. He was marginalized and experienced life on the fringe of the in-group in high school since he was from a blue-collar family and his dad was a bus driver. His private school peers were from the upper classes with professional parents. He was invited to their parties on occasion but was never able to become a part of the in-group. On occasion he was taunted and ridiculed by them. This caused so much traumatic anguish that he would vomit in the morning prior to leaving for school. He eventually transferred out of the school, but the psychological damage was done and was connected to his serving yips.

When overt rejection is experienced in middle or high school, patients will develop ways to "compensate" or manage the painful experiences. For many athletes, they discover a sport in which to excel to compensate for the shame. The theory of overcompensation was first described by Alfred Adler who suggested that feelings of helplessness and smallness produce efforts to develop superiority over others (Adler, 1964). This is commonly referred to as The Napoleonic Complex, where Napoleon, who was small in stature, overcompensated by becoming a powerful and dominant general.

My patient turned to tennis as an escape from his dread and soon excelled in high school leading the way to a college scholarship. But as they say, "you may be through with the past, but the past ain't through with you."

As Adler suggested, overcompensation works for a period of time, but with age, illness, or fatigue, these compensatory defenses weaken, and the unresolved shame or rage re-emerges. In this case, the triggering events needed to match with the initial trauma. As a middle schooler he tried desperately to please and to fit into his peer group. Now as an adult, he found himself desperately wanting to please his playing partner. However, his unresolved rage against his peer group conflicted with his desire to please them. This conflict resulted in the yips. Did he want to please his partner or kill him? He wanted to please him but was loathe to do so. Anger trumped love. The yips in many sports including baseball, figure skating, soccer, or golf have a basis in a conflict about wanting to please someone to get their approval but also hating them. A pitcher may want to do well so the coach will stop criticizing but the criticism produces hatred and makes them unwilling to make the coach happy. This is what we mean by the word 'conflict' in psychoanalysis.

Over the months we continued to work on his conflicted state and his yips began to resolve as he differentiated between past anguish and present desires. His shame was resolved as well as his misplaced anger.

Only when insight from his past was gained, could we develop a useful pregame process by saying things like "My partner is not my teen peer group" or "I do not have to prove anything to my partner. I am no longer a child." This is what is meant by the working through process in analysis and it cannot take place without insight as to the initial source of his problems. The player's past must be dealt with before the players present state can be fixed.

Psychoanalysis is often represented on film with the epiphany of a moment with a sudden burst of insight and then voila, the magic cure. As a result of this cultural meme, athletes in general expect that one session of 'true insight' or that famous 'aha' experience will have a full curative impact. This notion is as naïve as the positive psychology mantras currently embraced by the field of sport psychology.

One session of an epiphany is merely the very beginning of the working through phase of therapy. And this is frequently where one sees the patient entering a resistance phase. Following a breakthrough, patients often begin to miss sessions or come late as they unconsciously re-embrace their neurosis once again. Information retrieved during 'aha 'moments can remain conscious and available for working through only with attention to the resistance as it emerges time and again.

**Resistance:** Ralph Greenson (1967) wrote cogently about the process of resistance as one of the great foes of the cure. Facing and working through resistance is considered the sine qua non of successful therapy. It is often felt most acutely as progress begins to be seen and is expressed by lateness, missed appointments, scattered or nonproductive associations or sudden termination. Patients feel a deep loyalty to their unconscious problems and resist giving them up. Neurosis is sticky or glue like and it's remarkable that standard sport psychology texts make no references to this extremely common therapeutic problem.

In this case, his yips lessened, and he gained a better hold over his conflicts and his serves improved.

The case of this tennis player demonstrates the relationship between current on court anxiety and a distant traumatic experience which were repressed and returned as the yips. The use of free association led us back to the past traumatic sources of the athlete's problems. A tennis player that yips on their service game may be experiencing the return of some buried conflict from the past. This is never a pleasant sight to see but there is useful treatment if the athlete is willing to be guided through the interesting and at times painful process of self- discovery.

## References

Adler, A. (1964) *Individual Psychology of Alfred Adler.* HarperCollins Publishers.

Greenson, R. (1967) *The Technique and Practice of Psychoanalysis*, Vol. 1. International Universities Press.

# 8 An Olympic Sprinter who Froze in the Blocks

The term "like a deer in the headlights" refers to being frozen in place as a truck is barreling down the road toward you. The experience of being frozen with hesitation is common in sports and when this happened to a world class sprinter in the 100-meter dash at an Olympic trial, what you have is the end of a career.

This incident took place at the Olympic trials leading up to the Los Angeles Olympic Games. On this day, the stands were filled with friends, family, and adoring spectators. There was a slight breeze in the runners' faces as they settled into the blocks, the crowd watched, and the stands grew silent. This was the moment that John had spent ten years training for. These were the finals of the Olympic trials to determine who would run the 200 meters in the Olympics in Los Angeles. He was the odds-on favorite to win this spot for his country, and everyone on the line knew it.

To win these trials and to represent his nation would be a life changing event. He would gain the financial support of his government for at least the next four years. Added to that, he would have fame, a lucrative shoe and soft drink endorsement contract and his name on a Wheaties box. All of this would be worth millions of dollars to him.

As the referee shouted "on your marks" he leaned forward, spread his hands, and placed them just behind the chalk line as he had done thousands of times before. He could see the finish line 200 meters away, and as he looked down the lane, he felt his heart racing wildly. The referee shouted "set!" and he raised his hips in the air and looked forward once again. Then he heard the gun fire…and he froze. It was just for an instant, but he already knew all was lost. He was about three yards behind. To freeze on the blocks in the 200 meters meant you might as well walk down the lane.

Training for the Olympics follows a similar pattern in all countries. Athletes who are competing for spots for their country are usually sent to a training camp where they are isolated from the rest of the world and are trained, coached, given nutritional support, physical therapy, medical help, and a variety of psychological tips.

This process of isolation and training of the initiates is best described as a liminal space which Jung first outlined (Jung, 1967). The liminal space

DOI: 10.4324/9781003272465-9

represents the process that all initiates go through as they leave behind one stage of life and prepare to grow into the next. As an example, the three-month period between an athlete's graduation from high school and his fall entrance into college sports is a liminal space but what kind of help do they get with this transition? Often the answer is none.

While in the liminal space of Olympic training camp, the athlete needs the support and the guidance of a mentor. This athlete was offered a seminar or two on visualization and goal setting, but this was not enough preparation. What may have been more useful is if someone met with him daily and simply asked him to talk of his concerns which obviously were great. This failed opportunity to discuss any of the underlying issues meant he repressed his mounting anxiety, and the consequence was seen when he froze in the blocks which essentially ended his career as a runner and he eventually wound up working as a bus driver with a drinking problem, forever dreaming of Olympic glory, forever tormented by this loss.

**Jung and liminal space:** Liminal space is that threshold space whereby we try to transcend ourselves and get to the next step in our development. In dreams, liminal space is often symbolized by attempts to squeeze through a tight space to get out of one room and into another. This passageway is a doorway filled with pressure, confusion, and anxiety and it requires support from a calm mentor to get through it successfully. We instinctively know that Olympians have gone through the crucible of training and those who win gold have transcended themselves and have gotten through the liminal space to the other side. Liminal space is disorienting and difficult. In "the Divine Comedy" Dante needed Virgil as his guide through hell and purgatory to get to heaven. And athletes also need a mentor to get to the next station in life. The film "Chariots of Fire" was the true story of Harold Abrahams, the Cambridge University sprinter who won gold by hiring the special track coach in Sam Mussabini who taught him the tricks of the trade. Abrahams understood that one needs specialized guidance and support to get to the next stage of development.

Extreme anxiety produced by the Olympics is commonplace and can freeze the athletes with overwhelming tension, self-doubt, confusion, and hesitation. The way to manage this is not to rush towards the repressive techniques of positive self-talk, deep breathing, or visualization tips. That is only part of the process. Every high-level athlete that arrives at my office has already been exposed to the gamut of mental skills techniques. What is always lacking is insight into what is producing their underlying anxiety and self-doubt. They all need time, a quiet setting, sympathy, some empathy, and the chance to ventilate their concerns. One must patiently sit with the athlete, give them your ear, and ask a few leading questions such as "So how do you feel about being in the

Olympics?" Or "Do you have any concerns about the Trials?" Then you keep your mouth shut and observe what they have to say or do not say. If they are heavily repressed, they will deny doubt but if you earn their trust and are not too anxious, they will begin to describe what the Olympic Games mean to them and to their life. In this case, the sprinter had some concerns and self-doubt that were just under the surface but never shared in the psychoeducational sport psychology seminars. When they begin to articulate their personal anxieties and self-doubts, one has a chance to address these issues, and this is when their defenses begin to thaw out and fluidity returns. When defensive positions loosen they have a chance to gain some insight into what is going on inside, which leads to ego strength and only then will performance tools be effective.

Proper sport psychology for the elite athlete is a step-by-step process that goes through stages. In Piagetian terms, the athlete does need to assimilate information into their mind, and this can be done in psychoeducational seminars where they learn all those performance enhancement tools. What is more challenging is to get the athlete to accommodate this information into a newly formed identity and this is the purpose of liminal space (Piaget, 1967). A mentor is needed that is experienced enough to take the initiates into isolated training camps and prepare them for battle. In these camps, they are often given new uniforms, special diets, new running equipment and all of which acts like a placebo effect in an effort the give them a new identity as they emerge from training camp. Jung's theory of liminal space is a remarkable concept that sheds light on the mysterious process of psychological growth from one level to the next.

We all must go through arduous training to get to the next level in our life. Liminal space is sometimes provided which helps us to separate from the past, find a mentor and be given all the secret talismans that give the person courage to enter the next phase. You may recall how in "Chariots of Fire" Mussabini made sure to give Abrahams a special talisman in the form of a necklace to wear during the race. Olympians face pressure in front of millions and they will often use special talismans to help them deal with this pressure. They often can accommodate to the new experiences by taking in symbols of what was given to them while they were initiates during liminal space. Symbols which represent courage, bravery, focus, determination, will power, and pride. The pathway to growth and change in often mysterious and arduous and Carl Jung's theories of liminal space, mentors and talisman's are richly imaginative and spiritual and can be useful guides for athletes and the therapists who are charged with their care.

## References

Jung, C. G. (1967) *Symbols of Transformation*. Princeton University Press.

Piaget, J. (1967) *The Psychology of Intelligence*. International Library of Psychology, Philosophy and Scientific Method.

# 9 Anxiety, Overthinking, and Loss of Flow in a Hockey Player

Flow is that magical space where the athlete seems oblivious to all but the process of the game. Play is effortless, time flies by or stands still and they perform perfectly. Flow is the holy grail of sports and was first described by Csikszentmihalyi at the University of Chicago (1989). The question is why is this wonderful state so hard to find or stay with? It can't be found by talking about "optimal states of arousal" or some such idea. The following is the case of a 17-year-old hockey player who lost his flow and how we found it for him. He had immense talent, was given a full scholarship to a private high school, but then inexplicably played himself out of the starting lineup.

His parents were concerned that he was no longer enthused about playing, appeared stiff and passive while on the ice. They worried that if his problems continued much longer, he would be marginalized permanently and would put college scholarship money out of reach. And today that amounts to more than $280,000.

When we talked, the player described himself as being out of sync with the flow of the game and that he was over thinking, not fluid, hesitant and filled with self-doubt. He was a forward and playmaker and in the past, he scored frequently. Shooting freely, being aggressive, taking risks and being in the flow of the game was the way he played in the past but now he was locked into self-doubt and overthinking. Where once he was free, fun loving, risk taking, aggressive, and enjoyed the game, now he was stiff, slow, and worried. I encouraged him to post onto his bedroom wall reminders of the way he used to play and remind himself of this style before each game. This is standard behavior modification and had a good impact for a few games. The return of his former self was met with joy by the coach, the team, the parents, and himself. However, he suddenly and inexplicably had an accident during the halftime of a game by banging his head against the bleachers which needed stitches. This form of self-defeat is not unusual and is seen as a player makes sudden gains but then quickly reverts to the past as if they are resisting growth.

Following his accident, we had time to take a more in depth look at his thought process and his pregame approach. He experienced two distinct

DOI: 10.4324/9781003272465-10

emotional phases. On the night before a game, he experienced a strong sense of excitement, confidence, and power and told himself "I will dominate these guys tomorrow." But this overexcited powerful positive attitude vanished by the morning. When he first awoke, he would sense he had lost the excitement and confidence and it was replaced by a feeling of dread and self-doubt. He would try to challenge this anxiety and say "No way. I know who I am, I'm going to kill these guys today" but this was always met by a dissociated voice inside of himself which said, "no you're not, you'll fail, you're a fool, you don't deserve to win."

Upon hearing his inner dialogue, I felt Ronald Fairbairn's theory of the Internal Saboteur would apply. This patient's Central Ego was weak, but his grandiosity would get overexcited, and the depressive Internal Saboteur added self-attacks and negativity (Fairbairn, 1951.) This athlete was lost within his own unconscious and wildly fluctuated between over excitement and deflation, degradation, and doubt.

**Ronald Fairbairn's Theory:** Fairbairn's Object Relation Theory describes the human as essentially relationship seeking, and the mind consists of three parts. There is the Central Ego which is conscious and then two other split off and unconscious components including the Libidinal Ego which produces overexcitement and the Internal Saboteur which represents badness and misery. If a child gets overly excited by parents, they can be dominated by the Libidinal Ego which produces grandiosity later in life. If they feel neglected or mistreated, they will develop an Internal Saboteur which produces self-defeat later in life.

The question then became what to do. Trying to ignore his morning voice of doubt, by replacing it with positive self-talk was not working.

This athlete's sudden injury is a part of this process and shows that pushing the athlete into the cure with behavior modification will often lead to symptom substitution. When I rushed him into a cure with behavior modification, he had replaced the frozen passive quality of play with injury to sabotage himself in a new way. I refer to injury and accident proneness as a way of self -defeat in many chapters in this book.

Freud (1900) believed that dreams were "the royal road to the unconscious" and perhaps his dream work would lead us into a place whereby we could meet and address his Internal Saboteur. The following simple dream is from our 25th session, and its analysis proved to be the turning point in our work and allowed him to return to flow. In the dream he was playing hockey, but the walls of the gym were adjacent to the rink which left no room for bleachers, fans, parents, or coaches. It was just him and his teammates against their opponents. Nobody was in the gym but the players. His first association was that there would be no distractions from coaches, parents, or fans if he played in a gym like this. As we talked more, he revealed that during his year of being home during COVID he would hear his parents yelling at each other in the next room and ever since then he was not able to concentrate on hockey, lost his flow and over thought during games. The dream expressed his wish to forget and ignore the screams. Hearing the screams had been traumatic enough that he was no longer able to give full attention to anything including his teachers, the coach, or the game he once loved. This produced an attention deficit which placed him out of sync with the flow of the game. The same dynamic occurred in our work where he would rarely be able to listen to anything I might have to say.

As we worked through the meaning of this dream, the power of his Central Ego emerged once again, and the influence of his Internal Saboteur grew weaker as insight occurred.

We used this dream image to help him to understand what had occurred to him and how it shattered his Central Ego, putting his more unconscious processes in control. This dream helped him to understand why he played as if he was distracted and out of sync with the game. This dream expressed his wish to be left alone and not disturbed by fighting parents and by his own internally sabotaging thoughts.

As he gained insight into this he started playing freely, aggressively and with spontaneity, risk taking and more joy. There was less grandiose over-excitement the night before and less self-doubt the morning of games. And as we focused on the directive to play freely and aggressively, there was more consistency, less self-defeat, less backlash, or injury proneness. Thus, we saw the Internal Sabotage weakened with the help of Fairbairn's theory and Freudian dream analysis. It took a whole lot more than positive thought to help this player get back his flow.

## References

Csikszentmihalyi, M. & Csikszentmihalyi, I. S. (1988) *Optimal Experiences, Psychological States of Flow of Consciousness*. Cambridge University Press.

Fairbairn, R. W. (1951) *Psychoanalytic Studies of the personality*. Tavistock/Routledge.

Freud. S. (1900) *The Interpretation of Dreams* (translated 1913). Macmillan.

# 10 The Tennis Player who Choked because of Separation Anxiety

Choking is one of those taboo words that athletes and television commentators are loath to use. That's probably because it's the most common psychological problem in sports and no one knows what to do about it. So, if you don't utter it, and deny its existence maybe it will go away. But it does not.

The following is a case of a professional tennis player complaining that he lost focus when victory was in sight and seemed to choke all finals match away. He was unable to close out tournaments well and this was costing him significant amounts of money. Though he always made it through qualifiers he seemed to become disinterested, passive and lose focus the closer he got to the finals where the big purses were to be earned. He rationalized this and tried to comfort himself by saying "Well at least I made a check."

Backing off the lead is commonly referred to as choking and is usually explained by cognitive behavioral sport psychologists as poor management of anxiety and a variety of relaxation techniques are provided. In his book "The Achievement Zone" Shane Murphy, the noted sport psychologist for the U.S. Olympic team, discusses these techniques at length (Murphy, 1996). However, the reason these interventions seem to fall short is due to a refusal to look below the surface and into the athlete's past. Winning can produce an unconscious feeling of separation from family or childhood causing considerable anxiety and performance failures. Glen Gabbard is a psychoanalyst who has worked primarily with actors and musicians who choke while performing and has found that often their performance anxiety is unconscious and related to guilt over separation or shame over being too grandiose (Gabbard, 1997). We may postulate that similarly in sports, a win may equate with the guilt of separation from a parental figure.

There is universal use of teddy bears or transitional objects that two-to-three-year-old toddlers use in their efforts to separate from mother without feeling undue anxiety. Children adapt to separation anxiety by bringing a symbol of the mother with them for comfort. But if the mother is schizophrenic, borderline, or narcissistic, the natural process of separation to

DOI: 10.4324/9781003272465-11

individuation is frequently sabotaged by her and the person will grow up with unresolved separation anxiety later in life. This kind of separation anxiety can be triggered as an athlete approaches victory. I believe this is a common dynamic in sports. Victory can unconsciously represent a loss, not a win.

> Margaret Mahler's theory of separation/individuation describes the emotional challenge that children face when separating from the mother at about age two-and-a-half as they become ambulatory and start to explore the world around them. If the mother facilitates individuation, the child gains independence, and the ability to stand on their own. But if the mother is threatened by the child's desire to separate or needs the child to stay close and fuse with her, she will unconsciously sabotage individuation and creates an unconscious abandonment anxiety in the child. Later in life, this dynamic will then sabotage an athlete's ability to finish off matches because wins unconsciously symbolize loss of the mother. When this is seen, the analyst can be used as a transitional object of sorts, thus giving insight and permission to the athlete that winning is okay and will not produce loss.

This athlete was raised by a schizophrenic mother and abandoned by an alcoholic father at age five. As a teenager, the patient was the fulltime caretaker for his schizophrenic mother. He paid her rent throughout her life and would loyally visit her during her hospital stays when she was flagrantly psychotic. By the time he arrived in my office he was 30 years of age and extremely frustrated, as he realized he was not living up to his potential as a professional tennis player.

At the outset of therapy, we made efforts to create strategies to stay focused and in an optimal state of arousal, but competitive pressures rendered these interventions ineffective. This pattern of becoming defocused and passive in the finals continued but slowly he managed to become more focused during competition, began earning more, owing to a combination of support, ventilation, and standard behavioral reminders to 'stay in the game."

Then, inexplicably, during one tournament, he fell off his chair during one of the breaks between sets and was sidelined for three months with an injured back.

Over the course of my career with athletes I have come to learn that self-sabotage in the form of injury is expressed when growth begins to happen if the patient had no insight into his or her inner dynamics. This dynamic was explained in the last chapter on the hockey player who hit his head between periods. One can guide, persuade, and cajole an athlete with the use of the many performance enhancement techniques available and their performance will temporarily improve but they will always find a way to curtail and undo this progress either by dropping out, getting injured or getting sick. These kinds of accidents and setbacks provide a chance to point out to the athlete how their unconscious is playing a role in their self-defeat. He had replaced choking with injury. More often than not, an 'accidental injury' is not an accident at all. I will devote an entire chapter on the psychology of injury in the "Odds and Ends" section.

Techniques such as relaxation therapy, visualization, problem solving or focus strategies often fail because they do not acknowledge the athlete's unconscious where strong internal resistance to success, conflicts and the need for failure remains active.

Following this back injury, the patient became more motivated to connect his current problems with his past and began to talk about his inability to take in victories, compliments, or money. Winning meant detachment from the past which meant guilt and abandonment anxiety. I could see this in our work because whenever I praised him, he would discount it and say he was unable to believe it. Being humble is a virtue but not when it becomes chronic and forces one to lose matches.

His inability to manage success was also demonstrated with an incident where he had won $10,000 in a casino only to misplace $3,000 of it before he left for home. It seemed that he had to atone for the sin of winning by giving back $3,000.

His desire to win was in direct conflict with his confused guilt about winning. He needed to overcome his separation anxiety if he was to win again. He had shown me that he constantly lost focus, lost money, and lost health when he had victory in his hand, and this was connected to his relationship with his disabled mother who needed him and his presence. As this insight was gained, he needed help in developing a more solid and mature self so that as he approached victory, he was able to remain stable and not become overwhelmed with guilt, fear, and dread. In addition, one interpretation was particularly helpful. He came in one day and told me he had somehow lost $100 the day before. I said to him he appeared to have a compulsion to lose things like tennis finals, money, and happiness and that it may all be based upon having lost his childhood to a sick mother. This interpretation seemed to be a key which unlocked the prison door of his past because the following week he came in and said for the first time he recalled a key to his stroke, and he went on to win that event.

This is not the language of ordinary sport psychology. When he began to share these memories and gain insights, he started to use the therapy as a good-enough holding environment and me as the good-enough mother who nourished his self-esteem, encouraged him to grow stronger and more confident. As we approach our tenth year together, he is now earning over ten times what he did when he first came to me. And his choking has been nearly eliminated. This is the power of insight and self-knowledge.

## References

Gabbard, G. (1997) Vicissitudes of Shame in Stage Fright. In Work and its Inhibitions; Psychoanalytic Essays, Eds, C. Socarides and S. Kramer. International Universities Press, pp. 209–220.

Mahler, M. (1969) *On Human Symbiosis and the Vicissitudes of Individuation*, Vol. 1, Hogarth Press.

Murphy, S. (1996) *The Achievement Zone*. G.P. Putnam and Sons.

# 11 A Boxer with Mind-Numbing Anxiety

When the mind goes numb, bad things can happen. A twenty-eight-year-old professional boxer, ranked 10th in the world, came to me because he was underperforming in international bouts and the media had begun to label him as an underperformer in big events. During practice and when sparring with other world ranked boxers, he was unbeatable and was considered the world's best. In practice his style was free, spontaneous, intuitive, and fluid, but when he fought against anyone during real competition, his style changed into a rigid series of frozen movements with less creative thinking, and less spontaneity and he would lose these more important fights. He described his emotional state to me as "freezing up." His anxiety got to be so bad that before one match he fainted, and the ruling officials insisted he get psychological help before continuing to fight.

"Freezing" when under pressure is a term commonly used by athletes when they become stiff, passive, indecisive, and slow moving.

This high-level professional athlete was already familiar with the anxiety control tools such as deep breathing, positive self-talk, and positive visualizations. But these suppressive efforts proved to be ineffective, and he decided to seek a more in-depth exploration of his issues. He was a particularly good candidate for long term psychodynamic psychotherapy, given his higher-than-average IQ (It has been my experience that most high level professionals also have above average IQs).

History: His favorite hobby was chess, but he had never shown interest in academics, obtained poor grades in high school but displayed early talent in football and was soon recruited to play on an elite travel team as a quarterback. However, when he faced national level pressure, he experienced overwhelming anxiety, lost fluidity, speed, and accuracy when throwing and was suddenly cut from the team with the coach advising him to play on a lower-level high school team. His response was to quit football altogether.

This failure was traumatic, embarrassing, never discussed, and remained in his unconscious. My hypothesis concerning his current flood of anxiety was that competitive matches against other world class fighters triggered his high school memories of loss, failure, and shame and this overwhelmed his ego function. This flood of emotional memory produced confusion, cognitive self-doubt, hesitation, tension, and a lack of spontaneity while fighting.

DOI: 10.4324/9781003272465-12

**Freud on repetition compulsions:** In his chapter "Repeating, remembering and working through" Freud was the first to describe the nature of the repetition compulsion or why people seem to seek out and repeat past trauma in an effort to master it (Freud, 1911–1913). As an example, if one had a neglectful mother, that person will seek out and find a neglectful spouse. By now there is large agreement that past traumas tend to be repeated and that they cause anxiety and an overwhelmed confused state. One reason that sport is chosen by many athletes is that sport enables them to face and work through past trauma. But what often occurs is that instead of the trauma being mastered, the loss gets repeated, and the athlete feels weaker and weaker.

Sport is a macho culture but nonetheless, painful shame and loss from the past remain and impact future performance. In the treatment of post-traumatic stress, one helps the patient to discuss the initial loss, shame, and helplessness to gain understanding of how his current problems are being produced. This applies to sports as well and this kind of insight helps the athlete to resolve their past traumas and thus become less anxious, more fluid and creative in competition, regardless of the level of pressure.

Standard sport psychology focuses almost exclusively on current symptoms and tries to prepare the athlete for the future. Although that is commendable, it puts the cart before the horse. There is little effort to systematically explore the past, and in fact there is a disdain of it. Rotella exclaimed that Freud's theories encourage athletes to view themselves as victims of the past (Rotella, 1991), and this position demonstrates how sport psychology has joined the athlete in denying what the unconscious is doing and guarantees failure in the treatment. Conversely, depth sport psychology trains its eye on the past and how that past is playing havoc with the present.

As a teenager, this athlete experienced anxiety which led to his being cut from the football team. Often, when a young player is thrust into national level pressure, he can become overwhelmed since his defenses are not strong yet. Managing the young elite athletes' losses and failures is crucially important to their development. If they experience significant embarrassment and loss and it is not acknowledged and worked through, they will either quit their sport or the trauma will remain dormant in the unconscious only to reemerge later in life when a related situation triggers the earlier memories. In this case he did both. He quit the sport only to have this memory return in another setting.

A good example of a parent who instinctively knew how to manage their child's exposure to pressure and loss is Richard Williams who carefully controlled the level of competitive pressure that Serena and Venus faced as kids. The film "King Richard" explored that point in depth.

During one of our sessions this patient looked up at my wall and observed the photos of a variety of super star athletes and then he remarked "I bet these guys had stronger confidence then me." I smiled and said, "not initially but they all managed to face up to their past and that made all the difference."

Nowadays, young athletes are frequently asked to deal with massive pressure when they enter the national stage and play in front of cameras and the press. When big losses occur, their defenses can shatter causing a feeling of vulnerability and no amount of talent, will power, training, pep talks, positive self-talk, or prayer can escape this issue. Analytic work attempts to reestablish the athlete's sense of safety, confidence, and strength by helping them to recall when their confidence and sense of safety was first lost.

We spent time making the connection between his current frozen anxiety state and its source which was rooted in his high school shame, and it was only after he discussed these past events did his anxiety finally lessen enough to make use of the more conscious pre-game strategies of maintaining calm and confidence rather than be worried, anxious, and stiff.

The athlete must be helped to make connections between his current problems and his repressed past. They will need empathy and encouragement to recall the initial traumas. This builds strength and a chance to let go of immature teenage defenses and to learn new ones. In a later section, we will be addressing the variety of psychological defenses that athletes can learn to cope with pressure.

Cognitive behaviorists limit themselves to the use of the defense of suppression yet there are more than thirty defenses that humans extensively use to manage emotions including projection, humor, suppression, identification with the aggressor, sublimation, and more. Suffice it to say that in this case, the fighter came to me in a frozen state due to earlier long forgotten losses that were triggered during competitive matches and only after he realized this could he finally make use of interventions in the here and now. I will often say to the athletes "You may be through with the past, but the past ain't through with you."

## Reference

Freud, S. (1911–1913) Repeating, Remembering and Working Through, Further Recommendation on the Techniques of Psycho-Analysis II. In *The Standard Edition of the Complete Works of Sigmund Freud*, Vol. XII. Hogarth Press.

# Part II

# Case Studies of Athletes with Guilt

# 12 The Championship Boxer with Too Much Guilt

Guilt is a totally unconscious process which resides in the superego and oversees the handling of our moral judgment. The athlete has unconscious guilt, as do the rest of us and if he or she should commit an act which goes against their morality, not only will they feel remorse, but they will also find a way to punish themselves by losing. Punishment can take the form of accidents, losses, or any other form of self-defeat. The following section discusses athletes who suffered from unconscious guilt and how they punished themselves.

Years ago, a professional boxer came to my office asking for help in the ring. He was a rising star in the middle weight division, but he felt that something was holding him back from getting to the top. He told me he lacked the killer instinct. I asked him to try to explain what he thought was blocking the way and he said "I think I'm afraid that I may kill someone in the ring. I know how hard I punch and someday I may hit someone so hard I could kill them." Those in the boxing world still recalled the tragic death of "Kid" Paret in his title fight against Emile Griffith back in 1962. Death, guilt, and remorse are the shadows that hang over boxing.

This boxer's guilt reminded me of Floyd Patterson, the former heavy weight champion of the world who once remarked that he was too much of a nice guy to be champion for very long. Patterson felt his guilt inhibited his aggression and after his career had ended, he lamented that he was always the good guy while Sonny Liston took on the bad guy role (see *Fame and Obscurity*; Talese, 1995).

In this case my boxing patient had guilt about killing someone and our sessions therefore focused on this guilt.

Guilt: Sigmund Freud felt that the mind consisted of the id, ego, and super ego. The super ego is the seat of our guilt and is established by parents, teachers, clergy, and a variety of authority figures in our environment. Guilt enables us to live within society by teaching us the

DOI: 10.4324/9781003272465-14

necessary constraints. These restraining values allow us to control both our sexual and aggressive instincts so that we may function within the world and so that society can survive without falling into chaos. Our sexual and aggressive drives are powerful, and they require us to tap them down constantly. Guilt is the internalization of societal controls and is an unconscious process.

A review of standard sport psychology textbooks reveals surprisingly little mention of guilt yet sports like boxing, taekwondo, grappling, and football require that you overcome your guilt about destroying or hurting others to inflict pain and to win.

As I began to work with this boxer, I would travel with him to bouts on the East Coast and learned how truly brutal boxing is. After every fight, the crowd goes home but the boxers go to the dressing room where they are treated by doctors who stitch up wounds, dress broken noses and eardrums and often will send them to the hospital for further work. This is the nature of boxing. It is kill or be killed.

I knew of the work a sport psychologist had done with Mike Tyson, where Tyson had been programmed to override guilt regarding hurting his opponent with hypnotic inductions. It worked exceptionally well. Tyson was already a vicious street kid with apparent sociopathic tendencies so with the help of the sport therapist, he was given free reign over his primitive aggression. Tyson carried this so far as to bite a piece of Evander Holyfield's ear off. Tyson would parrot some of the hypnotic implants during pre- and post-fight interviews with charming phrases like "I will eat his children." Mike Tyson started to lose his focus after his beloved trainer Cus D'Amato died and after he fired his sport therapist just before the Buster Douglas fight. Tyson lost that fight, and it marked the decline and fall of his career in the ring.

Since I knew of the guilt reducing techniques used on Tyson, I thought I would try them with my patient whose guilt was inhibiting his killer instinct. Before matches I would hypnotize him in the locker room, remove guilt and replace it with messages to "kill and destroy." This worked extremely well, and he began winning matches in the first round. However, problems then arose between fights. He was like an unchained monster and was unable to discriminate between fights in the ring and real life. He became too aggressive in his personal life, and it appeared that through hypnosis, we had unleashed all his primitive aggressive drives and he no longer had control of them.

The use of hypnosis to suppress guilt worked too well and the athlete didn't have enough executive control to contain his aggression during his daily life. He took to getting into fights in his neighborhood. We were eventually able to gain control over this issue when it became obvious what was happening.

This case shows how guilt does inhibit aggression but if you remove it with hypnosis, the results are dangerous. This boxer became so animated during his victory celebrations following knockouts that we were told by management if we did not control our boxer after these wins, we would not be invited back.

The exclusive use of suppressive techniques like hypnosis are commonplace in sport psychology. What I learned by working with this boxer is that you can suppress guilt and create a true killing machine in the ring, but attention must be given to all levels of an athlete's mind. The wholesale use of suppressive tools alone is what Freud referred to as 'wild analysis" and is what many sport psychologists are practicing.

Positive psychology rarely mentions things like patience, building a working alliance or the slow building of ego strength yet this case is proof that a gradual approach to the patient's problems is needed. Churches, synagogues, parents, teachers, and political leaders are there to establish societal control over both sex and aggression. Guilt and self-control are instilled by these institutionalized authorities so that we learn to control our instinctual urges. When the control measures are stripped away too quickly problems will arise. Sport requires that the athlete tap into his aggressive drives but if one tampers with our self-control mechanisms too hastily you run the risk of unleashing a monster.

## References

Freud, S. (2002) *Wild Analysis*. Penguin Classics.

Talese, G. (1995) *Fame and Obscurity: A Book about New York, a Bridge and Celebrities on the Edge*. Ivy Books.

# 13 A Long-Distance Swimmer with Survivor Guilt

The death of a sibling usually has a profound impact on the athlete. David Jansen was expected to win the 1988 Winter Olympics in both the 500- and 1,000-meter speed skating competition in Calgary. On the day of the 500-meter race, he received news that his older sister had died of leukemia. During his first race, he slipped and fell on the first turn in the 500 meters and was out. Four days later, he fell once again in the 1,000 meters. Four years later, in the Winter Olympics in Albertville, France Jansen was again the favorite to win both the 500 and 1,000 meters but failed to place, and his Olympic jinx was firmly entrenched. The 1994 Winter Olympics was held in Lillehammer, Norway, and once again Jansen was favored to win. This time he did win gold in the 1,000 meters. He received the gold medal with his new daughter Jane, in his arms. She was named after his deceased sister.

This well-known story is not uncommon. The following case was referred to me by a family physician during this patient's senior year of college. Despite high level intelligence and good looks, John approached his studies in such a lax manner that he was in danger of failing to graduate. There was concern that he was using drugs and smoking to the point where he developed a chronic cough. In high school he was a nationally ranked swimmer but had stopped swimming competitively for some time. John was the first born in an intact family and thrived as an infant and toddler. His younger sibling, named Jordan, was born when John was three years old, and they had a strong bond and played sports and swam competitively together. When John was aged 11, his brother Jordan was hit by a car and died at the scene of the accident. At the outset of our work, he was in full denial that his sibling's death had anything to do with his quitting swimming, his lackluster attitude towards school or his self-destructive acting out behaviors with girls and drugs. He did not believe that his acting out behaviors may have been a way to enact punishment to himself for surviving. The 1980 film "Ordinary People" starring Timothy Hutton explored the theme of survivor guilt in some detail and won four Academy Awards, including Best Picture.

Helene Deutsch's essay entitled "Absence of Grief" (1937) suggested that unresolved grief will be expressed through drug use, sexual acting out, a

DOI: 10.4324/9781003272465-15

failure to grow, as acts of atonement for surviving. Following the death of a sibling there is often an identification with the dead sibling and a desire to join with them in the hereafter. In published material by Jim Loehr (1986), Jansen's sport psychologist, he described how Jansen eventually became aware of the connection between losing in Olympic events and losing his sister. When he gained insight into his survivor guilt, he won gold. It took them six years to do so. Dan Jansen was impacted by the death of his sister, and he displayed his guilt with self-punishment by falling. In the case of John, he quit the sport that he loved but that was not enough punishment. He also had to flirt with failure in school, and flirt with injury, and illness through drugs and sexual behavior.

The process of uncovering and resolving self-defeat and guilt took Dan Jansen six years and it took my patient the same amount of time. Lifesaving self-awareness cannot and should not be rushed. There is another patient I have worked with for many years and was compelled to get injured just prior to any fun trip. He also suffered the loss of a younger sibling when he was six years old, and it required years of work to free him from his life-threatening guilt.

Freud remarked that guilt was an unconscious process, and one of the primary goals of analysis is to free the ego from the punishing severity of the super ego. The death of a sibling will always have a large impact on the athlete and the impact will take the form of survivor guilt expressed as defeat. This dynamic can be life threatening as well since one of the wishes that survivors have is to be reunited with the dead sibling. Careful attention must be made during history taking to see if the athlete has undergone this kind of loss when growing up. This dynamic often explains the self-defeat, drug use and other forms of self-destruction that we see in sports on a daily basis.

## References

Deutsch, H. (1937) Absence of Grief. *Psychoanalytic Quarterly*, 6(1): 12–22.
Loehr, J. (1986) *Mentally Tough*. Rowman & Littlefield.

# Part III

# Case Studies of Depressed Athletes

# 14 Narcissistic Collapse in an Athlete

Winning and losing are an inevitable part of sports. At every event, the athlete faces the chance for glory and victory but despair and shame are also real possibilities as well. Ironically it seems that for some athletes, winning brings only brief joy, but losses can remain embedded within for years. When losses are not grieved, some athletes will become risk avoidant. The following chapters explore the challenges of loss in sports.

A Division I college lacrosse player came to my office complaining of depression and a loss of interest in playing despite being on a full scholarship and being the only first-year student in the starting lineup.

His problems emerged when he arrived at college. In high school he had consistently excelled, received much praise and little criticism but his college experience was far different. He now had a harsh, old-school style coach who would scream at him from the sidelines "DONT LOSE THE BALL!" The player took all these messages as personal insults, and they became internalized and distracted him from his natural fluid play on the field. He began to make mistakes, which led to more screaming by the coach. The player became angrier, suppressed the rage which led to depression and finally the desire to quit the team by transferring to another university.

What is the right approach in this case? Should we use thought blocking to screen out the coaches' rants? Maybe teach him how to control his negative thinking or teach him ways to express his anger at the coach directly and assertively? Perhaps help with depression with positive self-talk or medication. Or maybe I could support him in his efforts to transfer to another school as he planned on doing. My approach in this case was to show respect for, mirror and reflect on his talent, empathize with his pain and reminding him of his many previous accomplishments. Along the lines of Heinz Kohut's theories in Self-Psychology, my most crucial intervention was to attune to both his talent and his pain much the way a good enough parent would. I provided praise, solace and admiration and respect.

DOI: 10.4324/9781003272465-17

**Heinz Kohut on 'transmuting internalizations:** Heinz Kohut believed that mirroring was our primary developmental need and said that children need to be shown that they are special, and wonderful and that the parent takes great pleasure in having them around. During childhood, our self-esteem is established not by the parents' words but by subtle gestures and tone of voice. The child eventually internalizes this feeling and creates a solid self, able to cope with insults and setbacks because they have no doubt that they are loved. When this sense of solid self-worth is lacking in a patient, the therapist has the job of parenting which leads to 'transmuting internalizations' or the person's eventual ability to take in self-esteem. This is the repair process that must take place when working with athletes with self-deficits. Providing attunement allows the shattered ego to slowly mend itself and helps the athlete find the true self (Kohut, 1977). This relatively simple, if somewhat lengthy process, provides far more healing than handy self-help tips, positive self-talk or assertiveness training.

Proof of this athlete's ego deficits was shown in his inability to handle the tough coach but also was found in a dream he reported. His dream was as follows: "I was playing in a beautiful stadium with two big-name professional lacrosse players. It was amazing to be there. At half time, as I exited the field and entered the locker room, I found myself in New York City. There was lots of traffic and I saw my sister's friend Joanie get into a minor accident. I asked her if she was okay, and she said yes. I turned away and entered a Subway restaurant. As I entered the restaurant, I was back in the locker room, and it was time to get back on the field. I couldn't find my jersey and called home and asked my mother if she could help. She said no but as I walked onto the field, I saw my father on the sidelines with my jersey in his hand."

We then began to talk about the specifics of this dream which seemed to be in three parts. The beginning was him playing with his heroes in a beautiful stadium. This mirrored his high school lacrosse experiences. Playing professionally was his ego ideal, his ultimate ambition and the driving force in his career. His high school days were filled with magic and glory.

In the middle section of the dream he is in New York City, seeking food and sees his sister's friend get into a minor car accident. Our discussions revealed that in fact he is now in desperate need of nourishment that he has not found yet and relates to his lowered self-esteem due to the screaming coach. The minor car accident is his primary process attempt to express the mistakes the coach is screaming about and his healthy unconscious effort to sooth and forgive himself for them. This was not a big bad accident but only a minor fender bender where no dents were seen on the car, and no one was injured.

In the third part of this dream, he is back in the locker room and realizes he does not have his jersey so he cannot enter the game. He calls home but mother is of no help. As he enters the field, he sees his father with the jersey he needs. Dreams where a player cannot get into competition because he is missing a piece of equipment, (i.e., a golf club, a jersey, a hockey stick) often reveals that they lack strong enough defensive equipment and feel unable to manage the pressure of competition with all its inherent risk and anxiety. His inner self lacks strength and inner belief since he has not been fed either in the Subway food chain or by the mother or father. This dream suggested a defect in the self perhaps due to inadequate parenting. When he then realized he had no jersey (no defense) he called home to ask his mother for help, but she did not answer. This suggests some failure in support or mirroring in his past and therefore he had great difficulty managing the coaches' insults. Athletes who suffer with damaged or weak self-esteem have a hard time coping with narcissistic insults and need ongoing empathic repair to restore their easily shattered self and make it whole.

Narcissistic collapse often occurs when an athlete enters the next phase of athletic development where he or she is facing stiffer competition and they are unable to maintain the previous sense of superiority. At that point any criticism, whether from the crowd, the coach or teammates becomes a public humiliation. The athlete with narcissistic wounding needs a treatment which offers empathy and sympathy rather than attempting to suppress the affective symptoms with self-talk, deep breathing, or medications. The repair process is human in nature, not mechanical and does not require specific cognitive interventions.

It is very easy to mirror the talented athlete because they all have such obvious ability. Athletes look good, look healthy, and carry themselves through space with a graceful elegance. Invariably they walk with balance and power, are well tanned, have luminescent skin, very fit, have perfect teeth and bright eyes. All these impressive physical characteristics are hard earned through years of physical aerobic exercise and sweat. The therapist can mirror an athlete's power, talent, and strength by acknowledging this and making it known to the athlete. This is usually an effective beginning way to reacquaint the athlete with who they are and facilitates the repair of psychological injury.

Mirroring the athletes' record of performance and inherent talent is powerful and the athlete needs to hear these things. All of this must be done with genuine honesty. I recall taking a course in graduate school with Leonard Krasner who was one of the founding fathers of behavior therapy and how he said there was an art to positive verbal reinforcement and that it must be expressed with honesty. Years later when I was doing my post graduate studies in psychoanalysis, and I came across Heinz Kohut's papers on mirroring, I realized that both men were talking about the same process but using different models to explain it.

An interesting example of a "transmuting internalization" was told to me by one of my patients who had an uncle who worked on the Johnnie

Carson Show back in the 1970s. Her uncle was in the stage crew, and he oversaw pulling the curtain back when Johnnie introduced a guest who was waiting behind it. This evening Sammy Davis Jr. was the guest waiting backstage and before he came out from behind the curtain, he would look down at his diamond ring, kiss it three times and repeat the words "I'm a star, I'm a star, I'm a star." This was his effort to use a 'transmuting internalization' to remind himself of exactly who he was as walked out onto center stage.

Mirroring the athletes' basic talents and gifts is a process requiring empathy for them to finally be able to take in self-esteem when it is needed. Narcissistic collapse and the resultant depression and self-doubt is a common problem in athletes since their performance is so public. Treatment must acknowledge this and systematically mirror the power and goodness of the athlete until that time that the athlete can do it on their own. That is when finally, they absorb those 'transmuting internalizations' and make them their own and that is when they begin to believe their 'positive self-talk'. This is a lengthy process since they all seem to stubbornly hold onto their feelings of self-hatred and negativity.

## References

Kohut, H. (1977) *The Restoration of the Self*. International Universities Press.

Krasner, L. (1995) *Theories of Behavior Therapy, Exploring Behavior Change*, Eds, W. Donahue and L. Krasner. American Psychological Association.

# 15 Depression After Winning the Rookie of The Year Award in Major League Baseball

The winning of trophies or awards is a central motive for many athletes. The human mind can project into these objects a deep meaning which they rarely possess. In this chapter we will discuss how a Major League Baseball player harbored an unconscious hope that his identity would be repaired and permanently improved after he won the Rookie of the Year award. However, upon receipt of the award he fell into an acute depression on the same evening.

The following is a description of a single session with this MLB rookie whom I had been working with and how I applied Christopher Bollas's concept of the transformational object to understand his depression. The session took place on the night following the award dinner when he received his Rookie of the Year honors. During the dinner he was lauded and praised by his coach and manager, and this was followed by a series of television and press interviews and photo ops. Shortly after this the player went back to his hotel where he was staying and later that night, I was called. This turned out to be an unusual session because rather than being characterized with celebration and joy as I expected, the session was filled with sadness, anger, and disappointment. When I asked him why he was so upset since he had finally achieved his deepest dream, he simply said "All that work, all that effort, all that discipline for all these years, I finally get the award and what happens? I get a bonus, a handshake, and a plaque. Is that all there is?"

It reminded me of the Peggy Lee classic "Is that all there is?" which had the refrain:

> Is that all there is, is that all there is?
> If that's all there is my friend, and then let's keep dancing
> Let's break out the booze and have a ball.

It appeared that he was extremely disappointed with the evenings event. I concluded that this athlete was driven by a deeply unconscious wish for his damaged inner self to be cured by this award. 'The thrill of victory' vanished so quickly that he was in a narcissistic crisis and filled with sadness,

DOI: 10.4324/9781003272465-18

loneliness, and letdown intermingled with rage. This state is reminiscent of Kohut's concept of the damaged empty self of the narcissist and their need for the restoration of their defective self. In addition, I was reminded of Bollas's theory of the adult's quest for the 'transformational object'. Bollas's theory states that adults externalize inner problems and seek what he calls 'transformational objects' in the hope that these events will transform them into a better and happier person. For many athletes, trophies or awards are 'transformational objects' and they see them as concrete objects rather than as symbols of achievement. This is why you often see athletes kissing or biting the trophies. Although I am using Bollas's model, there are a few transformational models now being used (Grotstein, 2007; Ogden, 2010) which focus on the patient's ability to symbolize or give meaning to their experiences or achievements. Many athletes are alexithymic and have little ability to symbolize or give emotional meaning to events. Unable to symbolize meaning, these athletes organize experience through action only and thus are unable to articulate or internalize achievements. This is why you will often here victorious athletes say during post-game interviews "I am speechless and don't know what to say." And this is why some get depressed after a win, like this athlete being discussed. They know something is missing but do not know what it is. What they are missing is the ability to symbolize their own achievements.

**Christopher Bollas and 'the hunt for transformational objects':** Bollas believes that some adults seek regressive experiences that parallel a time of infancy when they were soothed, cleaned, and made to feel warm and full. In the case of this depressed ball player, the award produced little more than a shock that this was simply another day in a long series of days and there would be no permanent change in him. There was no ability to symbolize or internalize what they had just done and this produces great disappointment especially after victory. They then turn to activities like drinking, sex, or gambling to deny the disappointment. Similarly, the tears one sees from Olympic gold medal winners as they listen to their national anthem may be because it is dawning on them that "that's all there is."

Both Kohut's and Bollas' theory explain the motivation that drive many athletes. Kohut suggests that parental failures of mirroring produce a defective self which destines the person to seek out solutions to this defective state. Bollas does not pathologize this condition as severely but suggests that the mother ministers to our needs and transforms our hunger to fullness, our anxiety to calmness, our rage to ease, and our cold to warmth. These preverbal memories of transformation stay with us throughout life and motivate us to seek out a variety of 'transformational experiences" such as purchasing a new car, going on a dream vacation, or winning a trophy. These objectified experiences are sought for their hoped-for ability to change us into permanently happier selves.

These compulsive actions are little more than fantasy quests and their impact is temporary and therefore frustrating. Frustrating for the vacationer who returns home to once again face the grind of life and frustrating to my patient who just won a big award and suddenly realized nothing has changed.

The athlete's inability to digest their achievements is a common problem. Bollas would say the frustration is due to deeply repressed hope. Kohut would say it is a hopeless quest to seek a cure externally when it must occur internally with the help of therapy.

The danger with this vicious cycle of hope versus disappointment is that it leads to drug or alcohol use as the last-ditch effort to achieve this ephemeral transformation. People will often say that it is crucial to enjoy the journey and to enjoy the process and not focus on the results. This is true but very few can do this.

Winning, trophies and awards in sports have deep rooted meaning and deconstructing its meaning only comes from a methodology which explores both the athlete's unconscious and their past. Trophies are desired and this goal provides drive for the athlete. However, when they get to the winner's circle and get depressed, it's a sign that something is amiss. It is good to have a treatment that can shed light on this mysterious reaction. Without this kind of in-depth understanding and treatment, the world of sports will continue to be plagued with athlete's who are chronically angry, and depressed and who run to alcohol, gambling, or sex to sooth the savage beast.

## References

Bollas, C. (1989) *The Shadow of the Object: Psychoanalysis of the Unthought Known*. Columbia University Press.

Grotstein, J. S. (2007) *A beam of intense darkness: Wilfred Bion's legacy to psychoanalysis*. Karnac.

Kohut, H. (1977) *The Restoration of the Self*. Inter University Press.

Ogden, T. H. (2010) Three forms of thinking: Magical thinking, dream thinking, and transformational thinking. *The Psychoanalytic Quarterly*, 79: 317–347.

# 16 Depression used as Defense in Basketball

Some athletes adopt a style of play characterized by a lack of enthusiasm or emotion, apathy, poor focus, and a spaced out "whatever" attitude. The following case is a good example of this style of play. This was a 16-year-old high school basketball star who was on full scholarship to a private school and was already being actively recruited to play Division I basketball. However, he had adopted a passive and non-aggressive approach on the court much to the chagrin of his parents and coach. In my office he presented as shy, soft spoken, depressed and withdrawn. He did not know why he had lost his 'edge' on the court nor did his parents.

History revealed that he had a series of significant losses. His parents were divorced when he was 12 and his best friend recently died in an automobile accident. None of these significant losses had been properly mourned. His father was a busy heart surgeon, and his mother was a nurse, and she was so overwhelmed herself that she could not provide the son sufficient solace and acknowledgement of these losses.

Winnicott (1971) believed that one of the main tasks of the mother was to acknowledge and to solace disappointments and losses felt in her child. A mother's denial of disappointment is then felt as a lack of empathy and an abandonment by her child and therefore the child will grow into an adult who avoids any further risk of loss since loss now represents a loss of maternal care. There is significant psychoanalytic literature on why a failure to grieve will interfere with creativity (Meyersburg, Ablon, and Kota, 1974; Pollock, 1978; Kirschner, 1985). Athletes perpetually experience significant losses both on and off the field, yet nothing has been written about how grief in the athlete will inhibit their creativity and spontaneity on the court. Loss is a common experience in every sport and for every athlete, therefore resolving loss should be one of the primary areas of focus in sport psychology.

Arguing along the same lines as Winnicott, Bibring (1953) has suggested that the consequence of unprocessed loss often results in an overly passive approach to life, and this applies to sports as well. I believe a passive overly cautious, lackluster, 'pass the ball' style of play is frequently used as a defense to avoid feelings of further helplessness and loss as the player approaches

DOI: 10.4324/9781003272465-19

victory. This basketball player had become apathetic and non-creative on the court to avoid further loss. A hockey player once described to me this style of play by saying "In hockey there is an oval within the oval. Those inside the inner oval are playing hockey. Those outside the oval but still on the ice are just watching, they are not actually playing hockey." What I did with the basketball player was to try to discuss the losses he had endured in the past, starting with the most recent death of his friend. This had a positive impact on his performance. The mother needed help to become more accepting of her son's sadness and setbacks so that he could gain the courage to risk failure in the future. Over the brief time we worked together, he began to show improvements, but the mother terminated without explanation, acting out yet another loss.

The relatively brief time spent with this athlete was sufficient to see how athletes create and use the defense of passivity to avoid the anxiety of further loss. With care and sympathy, the athlete needs to express unresolved losses that have created these blockages. This process cannot be rushed because the patient must be ready to cope with the pain of loss. Over time they need to learn how their avoidant passive style of play is used to keep them away from further mistakes.

Defenses like passivity may help the athlete avoid pain, but there are far better methods than avoidance. The use of avoidance as defense in sports will result in a diminishment of ability, creativity, and aggression on the playing field. As the need for this passive defense is removed by working through their grief, one needs to teach the athlete more effective strategies to cope with stress and risk. I often use George Kelly's Personal Construct Theory by having the athlete model themselves after a risk-taking swashbuckling type of athlete. In basketball that could be Michael Jordan. This new defense is called 'identification with the aggressor' taught to instill power, aggression, and courage in order to inhibit any emergent anxiety from below.

**Identification with the Aggressor:** This defense was first outlined by Anna Freud (1937) and is defined as a way of managing anxiety by taking on the role of an aggressor and modeling their aggressive behavior and attitudes. This defense is exemplified in the Stockholm Syndrome where a victim is kidnapped but then slowly takes on the traits of the captor.

This case shows how unresolved losses can ruin an athlete's career. The typical method of dealing with these emotions is to medicate them, but this invariably leads to side effects like slowed reaction times, further loss of focus and weight gain, all of which are highly problematic for the competitive athlete. Athletes also turn to street drugs or alcohol for temporary relief from depression, but these choices often lead to even bigger problems.

Self-talk, visualization, and goal setting cannot penetrate these avoidant passive type defenses that the athlete has adopted to avoid further depression. It takes real insight into the unresolved losses and a working through of these losses for the athlete to once again find the courage to act heroically on the playing field. Internal resolution of losses, insight into why a passive defense has been employed, and learning a new defensive strategy such as identification with the aggressor are all part of an effective cure. It should be obvious that this process takes time and patience, traits that athletes and their families or coaches often do not possess. This results in premature terminations and yet one more loss to add to the athlete's list of problems.

## References

Bibring, E. (1953) The mechanisms of depression. In *Affective Disorders*, Ed., P. Greenacre. New York: International University Press, pp. 13–48.

Freud, A. (1937) *The Ego and the Mechanisms of Defense*. International Universities Press.

Kirschner, G. (1985) The depressive process examined in view of creativity. In *Depressive states and their treatment*, Ed., P. Volkan. London: Jason Aronson, pp. 71–91.

Meyersburg, H. A., Ablon, S. L., and Kotan, J. (1974) A reverberating psychic mechanism in the depressive processes. *Psychiatry*, 37: 372–386.

Pollack, G. H. (1978) Process and affect: mourning and grief. *International Journal of Psychoanalysis*, 59: 255–276.

Winnicott, D. (1971) *Playing and Reality*. Penguin Books.

# 17 Unresolved Grief in a Tennis Player with the Serving Yips

The following description of a recent intake session with a tennis player suffering with the yips is provided to demonstrate the way unresolved issues from the past can have an impact on present-day athletic tension, including the yips. This athlete was a Division I tennis player who came to me complaining he had lost his ability to serve, and this problem was putting his position on the team and his scholarship status in jeopardy. He described how he had lost his fluidity and his ability to serve smoothly, and his serves would sometimes get spiked into the ground or sail high into the air beyond baseline, much to his embarrassment. He had tried a variety of stop gap measures such as changing grips or serving underhanded, all of which worked for a day or two only to have the yips return with vengeance.

He had been given several standard behavioral interventions in the past such as autogenics, relaxed breathing, and visualization but with no discernible benefit and he was hoping to find some help before he lost his spot on the team. He was in a state of anxiety and shame when he made such glaring mistakes. This unpredictable loss of the ability is also seen in baseball catchers and pitchers who lose the ability to throw short distances.

His serving yips had started as a 16-year-old, and he was taken to a psychiatrist at the time, diagnosed with attention deficit disorder and depression and promptly placed on amphetamine and an anti-depressant. Apparently, nobody had thought to offer him a chance to talk to a professional about his concerns. The medications produced panic attacks, did not ameliorate the yips, and he stopped the medication shortly thereafter. Just prior to the onset of his serving yips, his parents divorced. He described his father as hot headed and volatile. The patient had witnessed many fights which included screaming and physical violence. As a teenager, he had many angry altercations with his father but eventually learned to suppress his rage.

His yips continued throughout high school and into college and his skill and ability to adapt to his serving problems allowed him to continue in the game. It is astounding that someone with this level of talent and with the severity of his yips that he was not offered proper treatment. The most recent event that prompted him to call me was the death by suicide of one

DOI: 10.4324/9781003272465-20

of his friends. This event overwhelmed him and shattered his tenuous defenses, and he called me in a state of desperation.

When I asked him if he had ever talked to anyone about his family's divorce, his dad's violent temper or the more recent loss of his friend, he remarked that he had not.

He noted that he could relate to a piece I had written on alexithymia in athletes which touched upon how some athletes cannot connect with their feelings. This was a young man who had suffered a series of significant losses including the family structure and more recently the loss of his friend to suicide. He managed to repress these emotions but the pressure of holding them down was finally expressed through his muscle tension. I have treated cases where the repression has caused so much muscle tension that the athlete locks up and can no longer make a move on the court. The treatment of this patient would consist of helping him to ventilate all these serious repressed emotional losses.

This brief case review is given to make clear that the yips are best explained not by labeling it as focal dystonia, not by medicating it away and not by providing makeshift behavioral interventions, none of which helped but instead simply postponed adequate therapy. The athlete must be given time to ventilate all his experiences of rage and loss which then allows his body to relax and to return to more fluid movements. As the therapeutic exploration process unfolds, one may need to use some suppressive techniques as well. I often choose to teach the anxious embarrassed athlete how to get in touch with his aggression through body language, and this serves to inhibit some of the anxiety. If they begin to play act as if they are a dominant aggressive cocky athlete, this can help them to gain control over their anxiety about serving, but this method will work only after they have worked through the mourning process and the underlying grief and repressed rage. During intake with these kinds of issues, it is crucial to take a thorough history, look for underlying grief and depression, and deal with that first. Only then will you have the hope of applying suppressive tools effectively.

## Part IV

# Case Studies of How Athletes Use Psychological Defenses

# 18 Regression in Sports Teams, or Why Players Act like Children

In this section you will see a discussion of both effective and ineffective defense mechanisms used by athletes. Sport psychologists are in the business of building defenses. Defenses are established to manage both external and internal demands felt by people. The way athletes defend against overwhelming stress will determine how well they perform. In this section I will present case studies of athletes using the defenses of regression, identification with the aggressor, identification with the victim, dissociation, intellectualization, repression, projective identification, sublimation, and humor. The first chapter will be about teams.

In sports, every team will function on two levels simultaneously. On one level they are the team that stands in front of the coach in the locker room and acts as if they are listening attentively to what he or she says to them. This is the team that the coach believes will be working hard to win games, will be cooperative and willing to learn. But there is another team in the locker room at the same time. This team is highly regressed, is functioning on a childlike level and sees the coach as a parent and teammates as sibling rivals. Every team functions on these two levels simultaneously and to date sport psychology has not been able to provide a comprehensive theory or treatment to help the depleted coach resolve these confusions short of trading players or quitting himself. The famed NFL football coach Bill Parcels took to bringing a baseball bat to his locker room chats to encourage his teams to listen. I know of only two psychologists that are doing depth psychology regarding team dynamics, David Burston and Mark Nesti, both of whom work in the English Premier League in Europe.

The foundations of group theory were established by Freud, but it was Wilfred Bion who created the first comprehensive and useful theory about groups and why individuals seem to regress and become so nonproductive when they enter a group. I will discuss team dynamics on two teams that I was involved with. The first was with a professional basketball team and the second was with a professional hockey team.

**Case #1** is with an NBA basketball team which had much hatred and envy. I was consulted by an NBA player who had been ostracized and shunned by his team and was in a state of depression. Problems occurred

DOI: 10.4324/9781003272465-22

after his rookie year. As a rookie, he was a standout player and was in the running for Rookie of the Year honors. Concurrent with this, the star player on the team was laid up with an injury that year and did not play the entire season. However, before the start of the next season, the star player insisted that my patient be traded and created a rumor that was used to rationalize the trade. The narrative was that my patient was difficult to work with and was a troublemaker. Stars often have great power on teams and sometimes their wishes are like commands. The coach was forced to trade my patient.

This event is best explained by referring to Melanie Klein's theory of infantile envy. Klein emphasized how envy is one of our most primal and powerful emotions and this star athlete acted much like an envious older sibling that has been dethroned, and he was consumed by the rookie's popularity and systematically set out to destroy this player. The rational thing to do was to embrace the newcomer and work together for the betterment of the team but the star's envious side dominated and insisted that the popularity of the rookie must be destroyed through slander and a trade. The infantile envy, jealousy and hatred felt by the star player destroyed this patient's career.

**Case #2** is the case of a professional hockey team I was hired to work with. They had a good record, but reports of strife were present. As I got to know the team, I realized that despite having a winning record, some members of the team were unhappy and were hoping to get the coach fired by playing in a lackluster fashion. Anger and hostility exist in professional sports. The players and the coaching staff were competent and accomplished professionals but nonetheless the players felt ignored and so unhappy that they are willing to lose games to get a coach fired. Their unconscious regressive infantile demands were not being met. I could see that the coaching staff was exhausted and drinking too much. During my team meetings they would sit in the back with head down. And when I interacted with them, I could smell alcohol. This was proof to me that the team was functioning with a Dependency Assumption with a wish to be nourished, fed by, and saved by the coach as parent substitute. Try as they might to be responsive, the coaches eventually became depleted and drank to replenish themselves. Using alcohol to replenish the self is understandable but rarely an effective strategy.

I recall being interviewed by the head coach prior to being hired and he asked me if I could do two things. One, would I be willing to drink with the players and two, did I have techniques he could use to punish the players for performing badly. This is the level of stress and rage the coaching staff was under.

After two seasons, the coaching staff was eventually let go, not so much because of a losing record but more because the players were so unhappy. It seems reasonable to suggest that alcohol or drug use is a predictable job hazard in the field of coaching since the coach must always oversee a team which will have regressive infantile needs.

So which theory will provide answers for these depleted coaches and their regressed teams? To date the only real theory which addresses group dynamics on teams is from Bion, the Oxford educated psychoanalyst whose work on group dynamics had a significant influence on the work of the Tavistock Clinic.

**Wilfred Bion's theory on group dynamics:** His theory suggests that when an individual enters a group, they experience an unconscious regression or pull towards childhood. Bion felt that group members consciously are dictated by rational thought and try to focus on the task at hand. In a sport, this means players focus on the task of learning, cooperating, and winning. But Bion theorized that the group also produces a strong regressive pull where each member becomes more like children based upon their experiences in families. There are three ways that groups regress. There is the Dependency Assumption, the Paired Assumption, and the Fight-flight Assumption. All three types of regression inhibit growth by producing passivity, laziness, and resistance to change. Dependency Assumption means the group expects that the coach or group leader will save them, and no work is needed on their part. The presence of Tiger Woods on the U.S. Ryder Cup meant that his teammate could relax since Tiger was here and all this takes place unconsciously. The second group position is called Paired Assumption where the group is assuming that two members will engage in passionate pleasantries and that this type of hidden flirtation will provide hope to the group and again induces passivity. The Fight- Flight Assumption suggests that the group has met to fight off something or to flee from it. This group wishes to be led by a person who can instill hatred or fear in them.

Both the above cases demonstrate the tendency of common regression on teams and the theories of Klein and Bion can provide valuable insight and support to the many beleaguered coaches, G.M.s, and team players who suffer in this maze. Bion's theory have been applied to the dynamics of many of the world's global corporations and governments but not as of yet to the world of team sports—a place filled with childlike acting out.

## References

Bion, W. (1961) *Experiences in Groups: and Other Papers*. Tavistock.
Klein, M. (1957) *Envy and Gratitude*. Tavistock.

# 19 How Athletes Use Psychological Defenses in Sports

This chapter is written in order to demonstrate how a variety of defenses are commonly used by athletes and how some are more effective then others. Tim was an avid tennis player who aspired to be better. His stroke mechanics were fine, and he was strong, fit, and flexible and he was willing to work hard at tennis, but he gripped his racket with tight and tense hands which hurt his power. He approached the game of tennis as if it was a mathematical equation and he believed if he could solve the formula, he would play better and win more. However, his over analytic approach was producing slower racket speed. As an engineer, he was cerebral, and intellectualization served him well there, but his over analytic processing was destroying his power, and relaxation as he played. In addition, his anger on the court was suppressed, and this led to bodily tension and fatigue, as well as a loss of fluidity.

History: He was the youngest and the brightest of five siblings and his childhood consisted of being perpetually punished by both parents who were alcoholics. Getting a B on an exam meant he would be physically punished with a belt. He responded to this mistreatment during childhood by becoming perfectionistic, graduated at the top of his class, and then went on to an Ivy League college and to a successful career in engineering where intellectualization proved to be helpful.

Anna Freud was the first to describe defense mechanisms in detail and defined defenses as the way we manage underlying emotions or impulses that are considered overwhelming or taboo (Freud, 1937). Up until now, sport psychology has not bothered to investigate how athletes use defenses and instead assumes that the athletes' anxiety is due to vague processes such as 'irrational thinking' or a 'lack of coping mechanisms', but the reality is that the athlete already uses a variety of unconscious methods to cope with external and internal stress. Psychoanalysis suggests that we all use defenses and that some are primitive and others more mature. Defenses can change over time based upon normal development, psychotherapy interventions or general gains in mental health. This case has been chosen to demonstrate the variety of defenses an athlete used over the course of his life and how the overuse of one behavioral technique to control his acting out led to symptom substitutions including psychosomatic disease. We all have psychological defenses to cope with

DOI: 10.4324/9781003272465-23

psychological threats just like we have an immune system to cope with biological threats. One needs to first determine which defenses are used, in what way they are failing the athlete, and then to choose wisely the way you replace it with more robust and effective defenses.

**The Defense of Acting Out:** Prior to treatment with me, he reported that while in his twenties he 'acted out' his rage with angry outbursts both at work and at home. 'Acting out' is considered a low-level defense and defined as a method of coping with stress by engaging in actions which prove to be destructive, rather than acknowledging and bearing certain emotions. We eventually came to learn which emotion he was unable to bear but we will ascertain that in a few moments.

**The Defense of Repression:** During his twenties, his acting out prompted him to find a therapist who specialized in 'anger management', a form of therapy that was displayed in the comedy film "Anger Management" starring Jack Nicholson and Adam Sandler. The process taught him how to repress his anger. Repression is a mid-level defense and is defined as the unconscious blocking of unpleasant emotions, memories or thoughts from your conscious mind, Freud first described this defense which minimized anxiety and guilt and predicted that it may initially be effective but warned that its use can lead to greater anxiety down the road. (Timary, Heenan-Wolff, and Philippot, 2011). This is precisely what occurred with this athlete.

**The Defense of Psychosomatics:** The repression of his angry acting out led to a variety of psychosomatic reactions such as hives, back pain, and irritable bowel syndrome. He had unconsciously enlisted his body to now manage all his repressed anger and anxiety. Psychosomatics is defined as a mid-level defense and is referred to as a conversion reaction or a functional disease where the body attempts to manage emotional issues that the mind is unable or unwilling to process. The epidemiologist Shorter has pointed out the current epidemic of psychosomatic distress experienced in North America (Shorter, 1994). Psychosomatic diseases are due to genetic predisposition, the need to defend against emotions, and to achieve secondary gain of medical attention and rest. This athlete had no choice but to adopt this mid-level defense since all his underlying anger and anxieties were not understood or treated and he still needed some way of expressing these emotions.

**The Defense of Displacement:** Displacement is the defense where you transfer a negative emotion from one person or object to another person or object. Like when the boss yells at you, and you go home and kick the dog. In this case, Tim wisely found tennis to displace some of his pent-up rage. Although he approached the game intellectually, his health benefited greatly by being able to displace his anger onto a tennis ball.

He over controlled his tennis game with complicated thoughts which only served to tighten his swing and we slowly replaced it by choosing displacement, a better defense in which to tap into anger and aggression. I have worked with many great athletes who systematically read negative media reports each week as a way of getting angry with opponents. They nourished their revenge fantasies and displaced this anger onto the opponents they faced. Mohammed Ali would taunt his opponents before bouts to provoke them with anger and he used this play act to invoke his own motivation to win. He would remark that he had built up media expectations to such a height that he had no choice but to win or be ashamed to death. These truly great athletes are always finding ways to get angry and then displace this anger onto the playing field. Winning is not an intellectual exercise, and it is not an act of kindness either. Winning is an act of aggression, vengeance, and willpower.

Years ago, I was standing next to one of my players as we watched the field finish the last hole in the last stage of Q School to enter the PGA. The 18th hole was a tough par four with water around the green. My player was assured his card since he did well and so we were both in a relaxed state of mind. As we watched another player who was right on the bubble try to finish, hit his ball into the water and lose all hope of playing on the PGA Tour I casually said, "Oh too bad for him." To which my player said, "I couldn't be happier." That is an example of a player who is in continuous displacement mode.

**The Defense of Intellectualization:** When Tim first came to work with me on his tennis performance issues, it was clear he was frozen in 'intellectualization' or 'paralysis by analysis' which produced tense muscles, and a tightly held grip which stifled his power. The defense of intellectualization is defined as how individuals deal with emotional stress with excessive abstract thinking or verbal generalizations to control their feelings of anxiety or anger. So, we can see that in the setting of tennis he did not use the defense of acting out, repression or psychosomatics but instead used intellectualization. His 'analysis by paralysis' led to his weak service games and was the reason he came to me. Over time as we made efforts to understand his underlying anger and anxieties and how he had been using a variety of defenses to cope with these emotions we came to understand how his coolly deliberate intellectual defense was extremely helpful in his profession as an engineer but intellectualization, repression, acting out or psychosomatics were not useful to him on the tennis court or elsewhere. Given his higher-than-average intellect, he had instinctively learned to control his anger with intellectualization, but he could see it was not helping his tennis.

**Intellectualization as Defense:** Intellectualization is a neurotic defense defined as the control of impulses or affects by way of thinking instead of experiencing them. This excess of thinking, without emotion is designed to defend against anxiety or any 'unacceptable' impulses such as aggression or anger. Great thinkers think but great athletes do rather than think. Intellectualization may be good for engineers and sports writers but not for players. Interviews with great athletes are typically mundane and vacuous. "Tiger, what were you thinking when you stood over that putt to win the Open?" "I was thinking 'I got to make this putt'.

Over the course of our work, we focused from time to time on his home life and how he had been marginalized there. As he had learned years before through anger management, he repressed all his anger at home and was unable to express his needs or his desires. This had resulted in him being seen as an easy pushover at home and was being manipulated and controlled by his wife and made to feel like a third-class citizen. This only served to increase his inner rage. It was evident that he was using rationalization by saying to himself, "Why rock the boat by saying something. It will only create World War III".

**The Defense of Rationalization:** In the chapter on the pro tennis player who choked I referred to the tendency to rationalize his losses by saying "Well at least I made a check". With the athlete we are discussing currently, he was rationalizing his reluctance to express his needs by saying it would only cause more problems. Rationalization is a common defense and is defined as explaining an unacceptable behavior in a rational or logical away even though there is no evidence that this will occur. We addressed this rationalization, and he became able to anticipate how to assert himself. Most of the methodology of Rational Emotive Therapy relies on positive self-talk to overcome rationalizations or 'irrational thinking." Rationalization is a mid-level defense and is problematic because it does not allow for growth in the self or in relationships. We were faced with the dilemma of how to help him overcome his fear of anger and thereby improve his home life. He began to anticipate the various consequences to himself if he did try to express his needs at home.

**The Defense of Anticipation:** Anticipation is a higher level of defense and is defined as reviewing an anticipated stressful event by rehearsing outcomes in our mind and telling ourselves that it will not be as bad as expected. The phrase Murphy's Law refers to this defense by suggesting that if you are mountain climbing you need to expect all negative outcomes and be prepared to deal with them beforehand.

**The Defense of Control:** The player continued to employ the neurotic defense of control which is defined as the excessive attempt to manage or regulate events or objects in the environment in the interest of minimizing anxiety and solving internal conflicts. This is a common defense used by obsessive compulsives, and he used the control defense by overworking in career and by over controlling his tennis stroke. It benefited him very well in his career, but it led to exhaustion and psychosomatic problems. It benefited him well in tennis in that he was willing and able to employ all manner of fitness and tennis aides to improve. But it also produced the lack of racket speed we had discussed previously.

**Underlying issues that were being defended:** I have taken the time to review his changing defenses and have not mentioned the deeper problems which all these defenses were attempting to cope with. Defenses are established throughout life based upon the variable stressors one is forced to face. Oftentimes incredibly talented prodigies in sport are thrust into high pressure situations and rarely have the defenses needed to deal with it. That is when their anxiety and the yips begin to be felt and why many athletes then seek our help. In this case, the athlete had an abuse ridden childhood where, despite being excellent both in behavior and in school, he was abused and had insults thrown his way by an alcoholic mother and father for no reason. It was no small wonder that he chose the defense of acting out when he left home. Throughout my work with this amateur tennis player, we constantly referred to the source of his anger and anxiety and by so doing he was helped to ventilate, gain great insight into himself, accept what had happened to him, and develop genuine ego strength. When that occurs, the athlete has access to more energy, needs fewer rigid primitive defenses and can try on new defenses. I hope that this chapter demonstrated to you the way that athletes already are using a variety of defenses when they enter the office and that it is the job of the therapist to understand which ones work, which defenses would be more effective and also what are the deeper issues that need to be uncovered and resolved.

## References

Freud, A. (1937) *The Ego and the Mechanism of Defense*. International Universities Press.

Shorter, E. (1994) *From the Mind to the Body*. Macmillan.

Timari, P. D., Heenan-Wolff, S., and Philippon, P. (2011) The question of "Representation" in the psychoanalytic and cognitive-behavioral approaches. Some theoretical aspects and therapy considerations. *Front Psychology*, April: 2–71.

# 20 Dissociation and The Zone

The zone is the holy grail of sports, that mythological experience where the athlete obtains perfect focus, steady energy, and calmness. Most professional athletes have found themselves possessed by the zone on occasion and wish they could find it more often. Competitive athletes are under extreme pressure, facing strong opposition, media presence and cheering or jeering crowds. Those that do not have strong defenses will be unable to manage the distractions and pressure and will begin to feel anxiety, tension, and fear.

There are some athletes who can defend against the stress of the crowd, screen out distractions and dissociate from the pressure. The most obvious aspect of Tiger Wood's persona is his extraordinary ability to screen out distractions. When he is in the zone, and you stand next to him, you get the feeling of being invisible. He has remarked that when he is closing out a tournament and about to win, he feels that time slows down and that afterwards he does not recall anything about the event or the shots he hits coming down the stretch (The Tiger Woods Story, 1998). I had the chance to ask him about his notable ability to focus and he told me that this ability was with him as a youngster in school and that he has always been able to focus very intently. Intense focus is one of the traits of gifted children and Woods used this ability to enter the zone at will.

I think that the general use of the term 'zone' symbolizes numerous condensed meanings including isolation, focus, confidence, separation from others and time eradication. All these characteristics are also aspects of the state of dissociation which is a high-level defense employed by some people who have high intelligence.

> Dissociation: Dissociation is defined as the ability to deal with internal or external stress by the temporary alteration of identity (Valliant, 1992). In rare cases, the person carries a diagnosis of multiple personality disorder, where they become a different person and refer to themselves with a different name and upon return to normal, they do not have any recollection of what the other person inside of them did. It should be noted that the only way for this dissociative defense to be developed into

DOI: 10.4324/9781003272465-24

a personality disorder is if they experienced extreme physical or sexual abuse in childhood. I once had the opportunity to treat a man suffering with multiple personality disorder in long term psychodynamic psychotherapy, so I learned much about dissociation and how it works. He had a history of extreme sexual and physical abuse and an extremely high IQ. As an adult he was a highly educated researcher at a medical hospital and during work maintained a normal persona and functioned well but like the story of "Dr. Jekyll and Mr. Hyde", he had another entirely different personality that would be triggered on occasion. This was a very difficult and dangerous case which required multiple hospitalizations and a team approach to the treatment.

I have seen the normal use of dissociation in some of the high-level athletes I have treated. A world-class long-distance swimmer once divulged to me in one of our first sessions that in fact we ought not have sessions three days prior to any big race because he becomes a different person. When I asked him to explain, he said:

> "Well, I act entirely different than what you see now. I am hostile, distant, aggressive, and use a different name. I call myself 'The Animal'."

Athletes who are in the zone are easy to spot. My family has owned many thoroughbred horses and from an early age I was able to watch how jockeys handled the mounting pressure in the paddock before a race. I noticed that the world-class jockeys would typically zone out and ignore the owner's verbal chatter in the paddock and only look at the horse's behavior instead. They had already entered the zone. On the other hand, I observed jockeys with less talent, listen attentively to our instructions and remain generally distracted and otherwise unfocused. And they do not perform as well when on the horse. They had not come close to entering the zone.

If one observes PGA tour golfers on a Monday, Tuesday, or Wednesday practice rounds prior to any big event, you will observe them walking slowly, wearing headphones, and remaining oblivious to the fans and the press who are there to observe them. They are trying to enter the zone or a dissociated state where they disconnect from the real world for a time and not experience negative or positive thoughts or emotions.

**"For Love of the Game:** The idea of being disconnected from others is the way the zone is described by athletes and this state was demonstrated in the 1999 film "For Love of the Game" starring Kevin Costner. The film was based on the true story of Billy Chapel, a middle-aged pitcher who threw a perfect game and who used his ability to dissociate to get through that high pressured ordeal. He used the phrase "clear the mechanism" which enabled him to dissociate, disconnect and screen out all the external noise and enter the zone. The cinematographer blurred out the crowds in the stands and removed all sound but the voice of Billy Chapel simply saying, "clear the mechanism.' It is common practice to have all the players in the dugout move far away from a pitcher as he enters the last three innings of a perfect game or a no-hitter. It is as if they all know unconsciously that the pitcher is in the zone and is not to be disturbed in any way. The pitcher is dissociated, and one should not disturb this trance-like state.

I recall that when my multiple personality patient said he was entering into a dissociated state, the room would turn yellowish for him. When he changed into a different persona it was obvious to see. His body language and his facial expressions were totally different, and he acted like and even looked like a different person.

Dissociation and the zone are different words for the same experience, and it is an experience that most athletes long for.

The question is how one produces this state of mind. The literature describes the zone as consisting of relaxation, focus, confidence, and pleasure (Ferraro, 2003; Csikszentmihalyi and Csikszentmihalyi, 1988), but perhaps a better strategy than trying to manage these four contradictory states of mind is to approach the zone by adopting a new identity for a short time (Ferraro, 2015). The athlete can be helped to create a temporary identity while on the playing field. Efforts can be made to establish and reinforce a new identity by adopting new body language and posture, by looking and acting fearless, cocky, arrogant, or vicious as they move about in the game. This is the dissociative defense in action, and research supports this.

In the mid-1950s George Kelly developed his Personal Construct Theory which was based upon the belief that humans can choose ways to reconstruct themselves. Kelly's work is neither psychoanalytic nor cognitive behavioral but more of an existential theory based upon human choices. He would encourage patients to act in a certain way and by acting and moving in a certain way, it elicited feelings of strength and power which had a way of suppressing anxiety and instilling courage and success. I use his theory to help athletes find the zone by encouraging them to temporarily establish a new identity while playing. This is what they mean when they say "fake it till you make it."

I know of many super star athletes who use a variety of terms to describe their secret dissociated selves. Perhaps the most famous was Mohammed Ali who constantly called himself "The Greatest." Ben Hogan called himself "Hennie Bogan." Another super star soccer player was constantly called "The Blur" by his coaches and I am certain he enjoyed that label. These temporary dissociated identities are characterized with aggression, deep isolation, intense focus, fearlessness, and triumphant pleasure. Such is the way of the zone, and such is the way of dissociation.

## References

Csikszentmihalyi, M. & Csikszentmihalyi, I. S. (1988) *Optimal Experiences: Psychological Studies in Flow of Consciousness*. Cambridge University Press.
Ferraro, T. (2002) The Zone and Golf. *The Online Journal of Sport Psychology*.
Ferraro, T. (2015) *How to Become the Alpha Player on the Court*. United Sports Publications.
Kelly, G. (1955) *The Psychology of Personal Constructs*. Vol.I,II (2nd Edition, 1991). Routledge.
The Tiger Woods Story video. (1998)
Valliant, G. (1992) *Ego Mechanisms of Defense*. American Psychiatric Press.

# 21 Choking and The Repression of Aggression

Many athletes who choke are afraid of their own power. They repress their aggression and their natural urge to defeat their opponent. Repression is a maladaptive defense for the athlete and leads to anxiety, weak performance, and defeat. When aggression is repressed, it produces anxiety, a frozen mental state, weakness, and a refusal to win. The athlete loses focus and acts like a deer-in-the-headlights, filled with hesitation and self-doubt.

**Repression:** The neurotic defense of repression is defined as the withholding from conscious awareness an instinctual urge from the unconscious. The ego attempts to shut down the aggression and the compromise position is felt as anxiety. For an athlete to repress aggression means that they no longer have access to their own power and strength. Perhaps the best way to understand the underlying cause of this sudden loss of strength is by using the Freudian concept of castration anxiety. This is one of Freud's earliest theories and has its genesis between the ages of three to five, where the boy begins to fear the jealousy of the father. This is called the Oedipus Complex and for girls it is referred to as the Electra Complex, where the girl fears retaliation from the mother as she grows fond of her father. In fact, castration was actually practiced in 19th-century Europe to punish misbehaving boys (Sarnoff and Corwin, 1959).

The following case will demonstrate the defense of repression and how it led to choking. This shy, bright, and unassuming but highly talented catholic high school baseball player was brought in by his father who could see he was underperforming in his sport. The youngster had been expertly trained since the age of 5, spent summers in Texas at baseball academies and was already being scouted by Major League Baseball. His symptoms included dizziness, shortness of breath and a weakness in his arms while at bat.

DOI: 10.4324/9781003272465-25

He described a choking feeling in his throat at these times. He was an excellent student and was raised in a very religious family.

There was a notable investment of time, money and expectation that was on his young shoulders. He had spent the bulk of his childhood being raised by his mother, an attractive educated woman. The father was an international entrepreneur, and his work required significant travel around the world. It was rare that the father was home for more than a week before he had to leave again. His mother was a demure, gentle, attractive, and soft-spoken woman of Irish descent, and she taught her son good manners, kindness, and respect for others. His private Catholic school education reinforced these values, and he internalized kindness, thereby establishing a strong repressive barrier against any display of aggression, arrogance, or pride. The result was that whenever he stepped into the batter's box his natural desire to win and hit hard was repressed and was replaced with debilitating anxiety. He was unconsciously dealing with the fear of the father based upon the son's unlimited access to the mother for weeks on end. In addition, he had been taught to be nice to everyone. His natural desire to be aggressive and dominant was being crushed by his mandate to fear his aggression and to be 'nice' instead.

A child's natural tendency to be aggressive and dominant is demonstrated by the following personal anecdote. When my son was about five years old, my wife, who was against gun violence, thought it would be a good idea to discourage Jordan from being too aggressive, so she gave him a toy heart rather than a toy gun as he had wished for. Upon receipt of the toy heart, Jordan promptly turned it around and used it as a ray gun. Such is the force of aggression that wants to be expressed.

In the case of this baseball player with anxiety, his father was a naturally gifted thinker and told the son that he ought to see himself as a hungry tiger at the plate and that the pitcher was his meal. I reinforced this excellent guidance by providing him with a series of articles I had written about acting like an alpha male with arrogance and cockiness when facing the pitcher. He began to adopt an attitude of stalking the pitcher rather than the other way around.

Our discussions permitted him to get in touch with his aggression more and more. I would use slang and profanity during our sessions all to model aggression and to give him permission to be the same way. He liked this approach and gradually he was able to replace his anxiety with aggression. His repressive defense was replaced by identification with the aggressor, a more effective defense. He currently is doing well in high school, and it is expected that he will be recruited into the MLB upon graduation.

This case demonstrates how repression—a neurotic defense based upon castration anxiety and overt messaging to be nice—can produce the exceedingly common phenomena of choking. With the use of some insight and the specific teaching of higher-level defenses, choking can be resolved. Identification with the aggressor was used in this case to help a shy and inhibited baseball player get in touch with his power and will to win and we will return to this case in Chapter 25 to explore how this new defense was created.

## Reference

Sarnoff, I. and Corwin, S.M. (1959) Castration Anxiety and the Fear of Death. *Journal of Personality*, 27(3). 374.

# 22 Gamesmanship and The Use of Projective Identification

Gamesmanship is a strategy that nearly all athletes use, whether they realize it or not. In psychoanalytic terms, we call this projective identification and it's an effective strategy used by many well-known athletes. Gamesmanship or projective identification is placing a devalued or weak aspect of oneself into another who internalizes this weakness. In sports, this is occurring when an athlete projects the weakened aspect of themselves into the opponent by acting dominant, superior or cocky. The opponent introjects these negative qualities and suddenly loses confidence.

**Projective Identification:** Melanie Klein was the first to emphasize this defense and defined it as an unconscious process where a person projects a part of the self into another who then becomes controlled by and identified with this negative and weakened emotional state. When an athlete uses projective identification, it exerts a subtle but powerful pressure on the opponent to fulfill the athlete's unconscious expectation. There is an impingement on the opponent's thinking, feeling and actions. This process is unconscious.

Here are two examples of how projective identification works. I treated a local golf pro who lost his strength, power, and confidence for a year after playing just one round of golf with a young super star golfer. He told me "I used to think I was a good player with a long ball but now, ever since I played with Tiger, I see myself as weak and short off the tee." The "Tiger" mentioned was a young Tiger Woods who went on to great fame and success on the PGA. It took just one round with Tiger to shatter this local pro's confidence and self-belief. Such is the power of projective identification. It came to be known as "The Tiger Effect."

Another example occurred years ago when I was following one of my patients during a PGA event and noted that after he made a birdie on the 7th hole, when he got to the 8th tee box, he literally took up more space,

DOI: 10.4324/9781003272465-26

thrust his chest out and seemed to dominate the two other players in his group. He went on to win that event. Later that night, we went into a high-end restaurant in the hotel we were staying at. He had shorts on, but the dress code required jackets and ties. When the maître'd stated that he was not properly dressed, my patient raised his voice, exclaimed that room service had failed to dry clean and return his pants and jacket. We were immediately seated by the maitre'd. This is another demonstration of how quickly and persuasively projective identification works.

I will discuss a case of an athlete who was far too vulnerable and too open to this kind of projective identification and explain how we reversed it by teaching him how to use this defense himself. This was an elite college baseball player who presented with symptoms of anxiety, nausea during games, numbness, and underperformance at the plate. His history showed that while in middle school he was the victim of bullying for having a big nose. His sensitive temperament did not allow him to defend himself during these episodes, so he internalized these feelings of shame and weakness. These affects remained embedded in his unconscious and reemerged when he started playing competitive baseball. His talent was considerable, but he found it more and more difficult to manage his anxieties at the plate.

The treatment progressed on two fronts. Initially, we revisited his bullying experiences, and he slowly expressed the shame, humiliation, and weakness he had endured. This introjection of shame was triggered when facing a pitcher. As these insights accumulated, he began to regain power and self-belief and he was then taught how he could use projective identification on the pitchers he faced. He was taught to use swagger, a cocky attitude, to act in a sullen, surly, unfriendly aggressive way and try to demean the pitcher. An alpha wolf establishes dominance by growling, direct eye contact and body posture and when the athlete is taught this style it serves to inhibit his anxious state (Kelly, 1955), and simultaneously it intimidates the pitcher he is facing off with.

This behavioral maneuver along with insight concerning his initial introjection of shame is effective and demonstrates the way insight must be combined with behavioral methods to extinguish anxiety, produce psychological growth, and enhance performance.

## References

Kelly, G. (1955) *The Psychology of Personal Constructs*, Vols I, II (Second Edition, 1991). Routledge.

Segal, H. (1974) *Introduction to the Work of Melanie Klein*. New York: Basic Books.

# 23 Sublimation, Creativity, and Fun in Sports

I am frequently asked to help an athlete find the joy they once felt in their sport. They recall with fondness when they were first starting out and enjoying their sport, but the fun is now gone, and they ruefully wonder what happened. This inevitably leads us to a discussion of sublimation or the return of the ability to have fun. Sublimation is the defense of converting unacceptable instinctual urges into its culturally acceptable form. For society to remain intact, it must prohibit the free expression of sexual or aggressive instincts, and we must learn to manage these urges to live in society. Freud contended that the repression of our aggressive or sexual urges produces an inevitable low-level depression in people (Freud, 1929) and that we are able to garner some joy and gratification if we channel our sexual and aggressive urges in a socially acceptable way. Sport is one of civilization's primary means which allow individuals to give expression to these instincts. A patient's statement that he would "rather play golf than have sex" vividly reflects this process.

Sublimations like sports provide pleasure because it allows for the expression of pent-up urges, yet you can scan the sport psychology literature and you will not find a single paragraph about sublimation, something athletes experience and a process they benefit from each time they play.

**Sublimation:** The defense of sublimation was first described by Freud who considered it to be the cornerstone of civilization (Freud, 1929.) George Valliant considered sublimation to be one of only a handful of mature defenses and he defined it as a process where a person converts the unacceptable urge to destroy into a more socially accepted form of behavior. Sports exist to facilitate this process and explains why there are such an abundance of rules in sport, a process which facilitates the release of aggression but also demands it be held in check as well. The powerful athlete must play by the rules or will be penalized or ousted.

DOI: 10.4324/9781003272465-27

## Case Study

The following case is a basketball player on college scholarship who came in complaining of no longer enjoying the game. He had repressed all his aggression and his performance had become flat and out of sync with the other players and he had lost his spontaneity and his creativity. He repeatedly remarked that he had lost his joy and was not having fun. He told me he used to joke around in the locker room and on the court. It seemed that his humor was gone, along with his aggression and his ability to score points.

As we worked together, I gave him permission to be free and aggressive on the court and that no one is damaged, destroyed or killed by his scoring. Sport is only a game; it is not a war. I was giving him permission to be aggressive and encouraged his joy, joking, fun, and scoring.

I related the story of the way Tiger Wood's mother gave Tiger permission to win in golf. By the time Tiger was 7 he was already traveling around the state of California and winning. Before he would leave for the events, his mother would get down to his level, look him in the eyes and say to him "Go out there Tiger and kill, kill them all." He would look back into her eyes and say, "Okay mommy, I will."

The famous Tiger Wood's fist pump is a perfect example of the way joy is combined with aggression in a safe way. The fist-pump move is also demonstrated by pitchers in baseball. It is punching the opponent in the face without punching him in the face. The joy of these sublimated gestures has been dampened by the NFL back in the 1990s when a triumphant touchdown was expressed by a throat slashing gesture. The commissioner of football determined that throat slashing gestures was going too far, and players were henceforth fined $25,000 if they did so.

Freud said that sublimation was the cornerstone of civilization and he recognized that mankind is a species which lives in groups and thus has a mandate to control sexual impulses and aggression. These two instincts must be repressed and then redirected to let off steam and to feel good. Expressing these drives indirectly offers man great pleasure and sports is a primary vehicle which allows for this to happen. And so, like Tiger Woods' parents, when I continually encourage and give permission for the athlete to express his powerful aggression in this way, he is helped to overcome his guilt, his anxiety about power, and returns to having fun and starts to win. That is why sublimation is one of mankind's greatest tools. It keeps us happy, and it keeps society safe at the same time. This strategy worked with the ball player who soon became the jokester once again and used banter and aggression to gain his flow back.

## References

Freud, S. (1929) *Civilization and its Discontents* (transl. Joan Riviere Dover, 1994).

George Valliant, M. D. (1992) *Ego Mechanisms of Defense*. Washington, D.C.: American Psychiatric Press.

# 24 Joking, Laughter, and Banter as Helpful Defenses in Sports

Jim Carrey and Adam Sandler are among the highest paid actors on earth which shows that humor is valued in our culture. It is estimated that about 30 percent of all television advertising uses humor. Humor makes people feel better. My dissertation researched the way children used and responded to humor. Yet the use of humor is rarely discussed in the sport psychology literature and to my knowledge, Dr. Mark Nesti of the English Premier League is the only sport psychologist of note who has written about the way joking is used by the athletes to calm down nerves and ventilate pressure in the locker room. Professional sport is a serious endeavor with high stakes so anything that can deescalate the tension is worth looking into.

Anyone familiar with a professional locker room knows that the atmosphere is filled with banter. Joking in the locker room is the way stressed out professionals express their pent-up anger or anxiety in an acceptable manner. Bantering lets off steam.

Freud was the first to address humor psychologically in 1905 with his book "Jokes and Their Relation to the Unconscious." He felt humor is pleasurable because it gives us a chance to express what is often not permitted to be said in society. When we cleverly express our feelings in a joke, we get a temporary sense of relief from repression. This release produces laughter, improvement in mood, and a feeling of triumph and that is reason enough to learn about how to use humor in sports.

**Humor:** Freud suggested that defenses are unconscious ways of managing emotion and can be adaptive. He considered humor to be one of man's most mature defenses and a healthy way to cope with stress or frustration. He distinguished between tendentious humor and non-tendentious humor, the former being more hostile and the latter being silly and more harmless. Athletes regularly use both types of banter in the locker room to discharge stress prior to games. Joking continually takes place when a catcher and a pitcher work together and between a PGA tour golfer and his or her caddy. The presence of joking and laughter in a tough situation implies that one can rise above a pressure packed moment.

DOI: 10.4324/9781003272465-28

Famous jokesters from golf include Lee Trevino who may have won his play-off match with Jack Nicklaus in the US Open at Merion on the first tee. He took a rubber snake out of his bag and threw it at Nicklaus. The crowd around the first tee all laughed in surprise and the 'harmless' prank so unnerved Nicklaus that he lost the playoff. Such is the power of humor.

Humor and light joking are one way of establishing a working alliance in therapy since it produces a relaxed atmosphere. The following case demonstrates the usefulness of humor when working with a billiard master.

I had been working with him for some time. He had fallen into a slump, and he was working his way out of it. During one session leading up to a big event we were discussing his problems and he joked "My balls are afraid to go home." When I asked what they were so afraid of, he said "They're afraid of the dark" referencing the dark at the bottom of the pocket.

The light joke about the ball's reluctance to go home may have been an unconscious reference to his fear of his childhood home where he was severely abused. The follow up joke that his "balls were afraid of the dark" may have been a reference to his own dark unconscious. This athlete's unconscious held many dark and scary memories. These issues were not addressed at that time since he was 24 hours from a big money event, and it is generally wise not to address overly painful issues in a lead up to any professional event. Talking about that issue and uncovering an anxiety ridden memory just before an event is like a dermatologist telling a tennis star, he has skin cancer just before he plays his first U.S. Open match at Flushing Meadows.

But weeks later I did refer to those jokes about his underlying fears of home and fear of his own unconscious and used them as an entry point into these meatier matters.

In "The Interpretation of Dreams" Freud said that jokes have the characteristics of dreams, which use displacement and condensation. Jokes, like dreams, contain important messages sent from the unconscious and the messages are usually difficult to decipher without careful discussion. Here the patient was able to condense all his feelings of terror from his past into this little joke about balls being afraid to go home. Part of the symbolism used in this seemingly harmless joke alludes to a fear of success and parental retaliation as well as a reluctance to please the father with his success. The value of jokes from the patient is like the value dreams have. They are both creative expressions from the patient and so when you discuss and interpret their hidden meanings, the patient has a more difficult time denying what has been expressed. Humor, like dreams, is an example of good mental health and it's a defense that is of use to the anxious, angry athlete.

Humor, jokes, and banter are commonly used by athletes and the psychoanalytic approach to their banter is the only theory I know that addresses its use in sports. Except for a single paragraph in Mark Nesti's book

"The Psychology of Football" I have not come across a serious discussion of this subject in all of sport psychology. And that's no joke.

## Reference

Freud, S. (1905) *Jokes and Their Relation to the Unconscious* (trans. J. Strachey). Deuticke.

# 25 Using 'Identification with The Aggressor' to Overcome Anxiety

This 14-year-old baseball player walked into the office with a frightened, deer-in-the-headlights appearance. I already knew who he was from having read scouting reports on him. He was an extremely elite level player but was in a year long slump. He described his feeling state at bat as dizzy with weak arms and shortness of breath. When I asked him what was going through his mind, he said he felt lots of pressure to play well and I had no doubt this was true since he was earmarked for the big leagues by the time he was 12 years old.

When one begins work with a very high-level young athlete in distress, there is an immediate urge to provide help and produce results. The athlete, his coaches, his scouts, his agent, and his parents are all in desperate need to find help. He had been exposed to standard mental tools training in many academies and this had proven to be ineffective. In this case, it was easy to see that the player was distracted by external pressures to do well and that this pressure had flooded him to the point of passivity and confusion. In addition, as explained in Chapter 21, he was using repression to avoid any feelings of aggression.

In psychoanalytic work with athletes, the therapist has two goals in mind. Firstly, one needs to provide some effective defenses that the athlete can use to cope with the inevitable pressure of performing at high levels. What is often seen in these uber gifted young talents is that their young defense systems have collapsed. The suppressive techniques are the apparent domain of the cognitive behavioral approach, but I believe their techniques are applied so sporadically and so briefly that they fail. As one establishes new defenses to cope with anxiety, one also needs to engage the athlete in an exploration of the reasons for the anxiety and the history of these issues. Without an understanding, and resolution of the deeper causes of the problem, no defense on earth will last for very long given the intense pressure of competitive sports. In this case we will explore only phase one, the building of a new defense, and reserve a discussion of his more deeply rooted underlying unconscious conflicts for another time.

Building a new defense: It was apparent that this young athletes defenses had collapsed to the point where he no longer had any ability to control

DOI: 10.4324/9781003272465-29

internal or external pressures. This left him in an overwhelmed state of dizziness, weakness, and was unable to breathe when at the plate. I recall another case from early in my practice where a 20-year-old golfer consulted with me after he had passed out on the first tee at his first international event. When I asked him what had happened, he said to me "I forgot how to breathe." Pressure can get high, and one had better have the defenses to cope. Strong defenses in the athlete enable them to handle a variety of internal and external pressure and without adequate defenses, the athlete will experience catastrophic anxiety, a state I have seen in many young athletes. They are tense, tight, anxious, panicked, dizzy, have dry mouth, nausea, and a variety of other anxiety states. All this leads to underperformance and slumps, no matter what level of talent, coaching, and training.

It is often not clear as to the type of defense the athlete is currently using but undoubtedly it has proven to be ineffective, otherwise they would not be in my office. In this case, I attempted to replace his repressive defense with the defense called "identification with the aggressor" which is another way of saying acting like an alpha male. This technique is similar to Joseph Wolpe's use of reciprocal inhibition (Wolpe, 1958), but rather than using relaxation or autogenics to inhibit the anxiety, I use aggression and anger which seems to be a more effective tool. Freud referred to it as the defense of becoming what one fears the most and I refer to it as becoming an alpha wolf. The alpha wolf acts in a dominating, aggressive and fearless manner when facing down competitors to his throne. The establishment of power and rank is typical of almost all species and has an evolutionary purpose. All species are essentially programed to understand both dominant and submissive behaviors. This phenomenon is readily observed in sports by noting the way a super star athlete moves and interacts with his peers. I recall a conversation I had with one of my players after he had played a round with super star golfer, Rory McIlroy. I asked him how it went, and he remarked "He was a very nice guy, but it was clear that we both knew who was in charge." The alpha wolf always acts as if they are in charge and in sports the alpha athlete gets the teammates and competitors to submit to this power unconsciously. Armed with this knowledge, I endeavored to teach this athlete how to swagger and stare and feel aggressive when facing pitchers.

This young ball player was a gifted and sensitive student, and he was able to pick up this attitude of aggression and it helped him to gain control over his anxiety by suppressing it with these behavioral attitudes. There is research by George Kelly done in the 1950s which suggested that acting a certain way can produce internal emotional reactions which mirror the behavior being modeled. So, if one helps the hitter to act with a cocky swagger and stare at the pitcher with disdain, the pitcher will in turn pick up on this attitude and may begin to feel a little less sure of himself. This reaction then helps the hitter to gain a little more confidence. We established this pattern, and this feedback loop allowed him to gain more control over his anxiety and replace it with an aggressive approach to the game. This is how I will often help the athlete to initially ameliorate the anxiety. Emotions are arranged into opposites, so aggression is the opposite of anxiety. The bipolar nature of these two emotions is seen in the so-called fight-flight response. I use this concept to suppress or inhibit anxiety with aggression. In psychoanalytic terms I am teaching the athlete to identify with the aggressor and not the victim.

Personal Construct Theory by George Kelly: Kelly was a psychologist who was not aligned with either psychoanalysis or behavioral therapy. His theory was more experiential and was referred to as Personal Constructs Theory which emphasized that humans organize experiences into patterns, that we 'psychologically channel' experiences by anticipating or predicting the behaviors of ourselves and others. He went on to suggest that if we construct alternative outcomes or expectations, these anticipated patterns can be changed (Kelly, 1955).

In the case under discussion here, his parents and coaches were convinced that the necessary work was done, and they terminated against my advice. However, when good work has been done and termination is insisted upon, I rarely fight this process but internally know that I will be getting another call from the family within a year or so. But for our purposes in this section on defenses, I only wanted to discuss the initial establishment of the defense called "identification with the aggressor.' As with all defensive work, it is only the beginning of what is needed, since the underlying traumas or conflicts remain and will eventually break through once again, no matter how strong the defenses. Furthermore, if the issues and conflicts do not break through, the amount of defensive energy it takes to suppress them is costly and exhausting to the athlete.

## References

Kelly, G. (1955) *The Psychology of Personal Constructs*, Vol I and II (Second Edition, 1991). Routledge.

Wolpe, J. (1958) *Psychotherapy by reciprocal inhibition.* Stanford University Press.

# 26 Altruism and Sportsmanship

The case I present to you is a former Division 1 All-American football player who demonstrated an altruistic attitude toward teammates and who upon graduation became a volunteer firefighter. I have treated him for over 7 years, and I've been able to observe numerous altruistic behaviors, all of which have benefited others and many of which have been of serious cost to him.

Altruism is nothing new to athletes. Most of the professional athletes I know are philanthropic and donate large sums of money to a variety of charities, yet they rarely get credit for it. As an example, K J Choi, the Korean PGA star, donates all his tournament earnings to the poor when he plays in Korea. Patrick Reed, another PGA star, donates both to cancer research and Ronald McDonald House through his Team Reed Foundation.

**Altruism:** Altruism is a defense that psychoanalysts consider to be one of the more adaptive and is defined as the surrender of direct gratification in favor of vicarious satisfaction obtained through service to others. Altruism derives from the Latin word 'alter' which means 'other people' and is defined as the moral inclination to help others without need for reciprocity. Altruism is a basic tenet in all world religions which often suggest tithing 10% of one's incomes to the church. Philanthropy, volunteerism, and charity work are all examples of altruism.

The compassionate concern for another's well-being has been studied by ethologists, evolutionary psychologists, psychoanalysts, and sociologists. Animals are often surprisingly altruistic, something I learned one morning as I was walking around my neighborhood. I noticed a cat stalking an injured bird and then I saw another bird standing in the street making a big commotion and flapping its wings in efforts to distract the cat away from the injured bird. That bird was risking its own life to save another bird. This is an example of altruism.

DOI: 10.4324/9781003272465-30

The compassionate concern for others rather than oneself is the definition of teamwork and team chemistry yet of the many sport psychology textbooks I have read, I have yet to find a single mention of the word altruism. When this football player was in college, he twice played with a broken hand which was extremely painful, but since he played such a key role, the games that he stayed in produced national championships for his team. His altruism did not stop in college. When he acquired work after college in the world of finance, he also felt it was important to become a volunteer firefighter and did all the training which was required. Furthermore, each year he does a 'stair climb' to remember those who sacrificed their lives in the 9/11 attacks.

His altruistic sacrifice for the good of others is the perfect demonstration of being a 'team player' and makes him the opposite of a narcissist.

How did he acquire this defense? Is it healthy or are there times when this defense becomes self-destructive? Can this trait be taught to other players to improve teamwork?

Altruism, like all defenses, is developed to manage anxiety. If one harbors self-doubt, or shame, or if one has been discriminated against then doing altruistic deeds is a prosocial way of handling it by proving to yourself and to others that you are worthy of love. Altruism is a good way to deal with that self-doubt.

Altruism is often a good thing but like anything else, too much of it can produce burnout, resentment or even bankruptcy. I know of one patient who threw away $300,000 on very questionable charity requests. And that was $300,000 that he could not afford to give away. The term for this is pathological altruism.

An altruistic attitude towards a team is valuable but can it be taught? To teach a new defense, one must first understand the defense currently in use. Bion's work on group dynamics predicts that the primitive defenses of acting out, selfishness, envy and regression are virtually universal in groups. So, the team leader or coach first needs to point out and interpret the acting out and regressive defenses and explain why they are being used. This is no small task.

As these interpretations are taking place, the new defense system needs to be discussed, and the players need to understand the value of altruism to motivate them to adopt this value system. There are two films with famous half-time football speeches that emphasized the concept of altruistic giving to teammates. Billy Bob Thorton's speech in the film "Friday Night Lights" and Al Pacino's speech in the film "Any Given Sunday" both implored the players to give selflessly to the team. But how does one convince players to do this.

A study on the health benefits contained within an altruistic environment offers valuable and persuasive information. A study which emphasizes the value of true cooperation was done by the epidemiologists Wolf and Bruhn and published in *The Power of Clan: The Influence of Human Relationships on Heart Disease* (1993). In the 1960s, these epidemiologists from Temple

University happened to meet a local physician from Roseto, Pennsylvania who told them that there was virtually no heart disease or diabetes in Roseto, a town populated primarily by Italian immigrants from Roseto, Italy. They discovered that despite habits of smoking, drinking, and eating all the wrong foods, this town seemed to be immune to all the diseases of modern civilization including heart disease and diabetes. This led to several teams of medical researchers over the next 25 years who descended upon Roseto to study the social reasons that seemed to insure the health and longevity of this clan. The essence of the findings from various groups of researchers over three decades was that the values of mutual respect and cooperation found in Roseto insured longevity, happiness, and health. In contrast, other towns located nearby were more Americanized, individualistic, competitive, fast moving, and materialistic and these people died sooner and had more modern diseases of stress.

These findings are worth considering when making efforts to teach the value of cooperation and teamwork to sports franchises. We live in a world of selfishness and self-interest but strangely enough, cooperation and altruism are the secret sauce that makes teams win. My patient was a good example of the power of giving.

## Reference

Wolf, S and Bruhn J. (1993) *The Power of Clan; The Influence of Human Relationships on Heart Disease.* Transaction Publishers.

# Part V

# Case Studies of The Way Birth Order Influences an Athlete's Performance

# 27 The First-Born Child, The Scars of Dethronement and Fear of Failure

Birth order plays a surprisingly dramatic role in sports performance. If you're an only child, a middle child, the youngest or a twin, your early childhood experience will have a significant influence on success or failure on the playing field based upon inevitable psychological patterning that has occurred throughout the early years. This section explores real life examples from each position in birth order.

The first case concerns a good amateur tennis player who said his anxiety in tennis was a problem. In addition, he was hesitant regarding the launching of his new business enterprise. He was a financial advisor and was employed by a major hedge fund, but, based upon his ability, he felt he was ready to launch his own business but was stalled in the development phase for two years. He was concerned about this stagnation and described himself as 'frozen' in his attempts to progress. In this chapter, we shall focus on the issue of birth order and how it was producing his stagnation of growth and work inhibition.

**History:** His childhood history showed that he was the older of two siblings with his younger sister born when he was four-and-a-half years old. He was a gifted child who was adorable to look at, walked and spoke early and learned to read by age four, and his giftedness garnered him continuous family praise. Shortly before his fifth birthday his sister was born, and her arrival produced a severe regression in him. He became angry, developed tantrums, and even reverted to soiling his pants again. This dethronement was traumatic. When he entered school, it was evident that he was a gifted student and excelled. By the fourth grade he was labeled 'boy genius' and performed at the top of his class. But as he became more socially aware in about 5th grade and felt it was not 'cool' to be too smart, he began to ignore his schoolwork to become socially accepted by being a part of the 'cool kids' who never studied.

This characterized the remainder of his academic life. Upon graduating from college, he landed a job working in sales, improved his tennis game and moved up in the finance world. This is when he called me ostensibly because he suffered from anger and anxiety in tennis.

**Course of therapy:** He was initially given the standard tools for anger control which included basic self- talk regarding forgiveness. In addition, we

DOI: 10.4324/9781003272465-32

discussed the causes of his anxiety in tennis but, as is often the case, the anxiety control proved to be more problematic to suppress. Since he only played tennis twice per week, his expectation to be an excellent player was unrealistic. In addition, since he was not in any serious quest to obtain wins in tennis, our discussions turned to other concerns. It was in the business area that his frozen quality came to the fore. He had reached a roadblock regarding the launching of his new business. He would describe this problem as being 'frozen in ice' and as we discussed this, it became clear that he was terrified his business efforts may fail and that he was unconsciously procrastinating to avoid experiencing the possibility of failure and the shattering of his dream.

His fear and hesitation began to remind me of the well-known British nursery rhyme Humpty Dumpty which was popularized in Lewis Carroll's *Through a Looking Glass*. Humpty Dumpty had a great fall and all the king's horses, and all the king's men could not put Humpty together again. This patient was just like Humpty Dumpty with an enormous fear that if he failed in his new enterprise, he would shatter and not be able to put himself back together again.

This rhyme remains so popular throughout world culture because it references a failure, a dethroning, and the shattering of identity.

As our work progressed, we set up timelines and deadlines to complete the various tasks necessary to start up a business and I provided encouragement along the way. All these interventions are the usual fare in sport and behavioral therapy, yet the underlying blockages, procrastination and fears remained.

**Traits of the First Born:** According to Alfred Adler first borns all have a common experience of being dethroned, must learn to share, have high expectations placed upon them, are expected to set good examples and become authoritarian and tend to follow rules and be strict. They often have the most emotional problems in the family.

He was a bright patient and his style of interacting with me was notable. Whenever I used psychoanalytic terms such as the "unconscious" or "super ego attacks", he would conscientiously look these up and would ask me about them in the next session. This trait of being super conscientious and intellectual are part of what Alfred Adler described as the first-born personality which they develop as an overcompensation for being dethroned by the second born. This insight led us back to his childhood experience of defeat and dethronement when his younger sister arrived home and the way he regressed.

His unresolved dethroning produced a type of shell, like Humpty Dumpty, where appearances became crucial, and this grandiose veneer explained why he gave up on academic excellence by grade 5 to be seen as cool. In his adult life, he made ill-advised choices in women dictated more by their appearance than by their substance or character.

The dethroning of one's status and the consequent loss which occurs at a critical developmental stage has great bearing later in life and hampers most efforts at creative functioning.

Adler believed, as Freud did, that understanding childhood experiences were crucial to help the adult suffering with inhibitory anxiety. This patient came to me with performance anxiety issues both in tennis and business and the most useful and curative thing we did was to uncover how his initial unresolved dethroning as the first-born child led to an inhibition of creative function later in life. If these types of traumatic losses remain unresolved, the talented patient will never be able to fulfill true potential out of a fear of risk taking and fear of failure. In this case, we slowly worked on his earliest experiences related to birth order and over a period of five years he became much more 'unfrozen', opened his new business, and became more able to take reasonable risks. His earning has increased by a factor of three and he is still seen in long term insight oriented supportive psychotherapy.

## Reference

Adler, A. (1964) *Individual Psychology of Alfred Adler.* Harper Collins.

# 28 The Middle Child Syndrome in a Baseball Player with the Throwing Yips

Jane was a 15-year-old high school softball player living in San Diego, California. Her father brought her to the session and reported that his daughter wanted to make the elite travel softball team but had the throwing yips. She was a very talented pitcher and had dreamed of making this elite travel team for many years. At this point her older brother attended a university in California where he played baseball for his college team.

As intake sessions unfolded, we discovered that Jane had a severe case of the yips where she would think very negatively and anxiously when throwing from short distances. Any other length throw was not problematic, and the rest of her game was very solid. The problem of yips in baseball players throwing short distances is a common expression of anxiety and it ended Chuck Knoblauch's baseball career as a Golden Gloves second basement when he played for the Yankees. My patients' throwing yips were obvious enough that any coach who evaluated her was aware of the issue, but she was determined to tryout and to make the team and this determination led them to my office in search of answers. The tryouts were a mere ten weeks away, so I wondered to myself if this was enough time.

Jane was a young woman, 5'10" in stature, athletic in appearance and had the grace of an elite athlete. Her grades were all A's and she was able to pass her classes with ease. She was kind and gracious in demeanor, had many friends, was socially accepted but constantly anxious and worried. I diagnosed her with obsessive compulsive disorder.

**Therapy process:** Over the first few weeks we became familiar with the gravity of her throwing yips. She feared the yips and the resultant shame it would cause, and this would tighten her body and inevitably led to throwing balls into the dirt and a loss of speed and control.

Our initial efforts involved standard self-talk, and behavioral interventions including use of George Kelly's work with body language to tap into her power and aggressive athleticism. This had a moderate short-term impact. I initially teach them so that after we discover the underlying source of the anxiety, these techniques will be revisited and employed with greater effectiveness.

About the 6th session I was still unclear as to what direction to explore to find the source of her self-defeat and wondered aloud if perhaps her older

DOI: 10.4324/9781003272465-33

brother was the source. Jane had described him as a good older brother but upon further discussion she began to divulge how intense the sibling rivalry was. When they were in latency age and played board games if Jane was to win a game, her older brother had the habit of punching her or pinching her causing Jane to eventually flinch and duck after any win. When they played basketball in the back yard if Jane would make a critical point her older brother, would intentionally knock her over. These early childhood traumatic moments were probably part of the cause of her performance yips. Her unconscious approach was to avoid winning at all costs because it will result in being beaten up and hurt.

**Adler on Birth Order and Sibling Rivalry:** The power of Alfred Adler's theories derive from their simplicity. He was the first analyst to discuss birth order and its influence on character and suggested that the middle child is often seen as an intruder by the older sibling. This case study demonstrates how the chronic attacks endured by the younger sibling can result in a fear that success will produce a physical attack. Adler described the middle child as feeling neglected and thus overly competitive as well. This puts the middle child in a quandary. They need to succeed but fear attack if they do so. This patient was very driven to succeed to garner some attention from the father and was mightily disappointed when she failed to do so. The middle child's character is also thought to be mild mannered in that they have learned to acquiesce to the older sibling as well as the younger sibling. This patient was mild mannered and soft spoken as Adler would predict.

I began to make these interpretations, connecting her yips in the present to her past traumas with her brother. Jane admitted that she always felt it was dangerous to win and tried to finish under the radar. I remarked that when she threw, she was possessed by her childhood self, ready to be hit by a fist. Who wouldn't flinch over this?

Correct interpretations are like epiphanies but unlike the epiphanies seen in movies, these epiphanies need to be worked through over many weeks and months. The working through phase consists of using insight from the past to establish a verbal narrative of how it connects to the current symptoms and then replacing this narrative with a more mature healthy one.

This is an arduous and interesting process. The weakness of Albert Ellis's Rational Emotive Therapy is that Ellis and the cognitive behaviorists spend little time exploring the patient's past and systematically minimize the power of unconscious emotions. I have sat in on many seminars where he was the leader and Ellis would ask the patient to verbalize his 'false beliefs, discuss the consequences and then replace these false beliefs with rational ones. If he were treating this patient, he would be asking "What is your irrational fear of yipping?" And Jane would have said, "I will not make the team and that will destroy me" or "I will be so ashamed I will die?" Ellis would have suggested Jane learn to say, "I will be very disappointed by not making the team" or "I will be embarrassed but it will not kill me." And this process would essentially be useless because it does not penetrate the patient's unconscious which acts like an ever present shadow. It would not persuade the athlete of anything except that sport psychology is an ineffective waste of time, and her yips would continue unabated. This is because the mechanistic use of self-talk by repeating it over and over inevitably becomes meaningless and stale.

I believe that the initial source of the athlete's current problem must be seen and worked through over time. The work of understanding the childhood fears of the older brother must be engaged in repeatedly not just once because any epiphany or any RET mantra will be swamped by the habit of fear that is now entrenched in her mind, her body, and her game.

The patient needed help in understanding that no harm will come to her if she throws a good pitch. No brother is about to emerge from the dugout to punch her. And this insight must be approached from numerous angles.

The connection of the past to the present remains the essential contribution of psychoanalysis and the reason why the unconscious must be dealt with. Random use of cognitive therapy runs dry and gets boring very fast because the patient as well as the therapist both understand on some level that self-talk is essentially an ahistorical treatment unrelated to the truth, the personality, or their life story.

This case demonstrates how birth order and sibling rivalry is influential and why the contribution of Alfred Adler is so profound. I would suggest that many athletes that play competitive sports are somehow struggling with what occurred to them at the hands of a sibling in the family. This relationship is unconsciously triggered in sport as you face your opponent who reminds you of a sibling. In psychoanalysis this is called transference and it prompts a regression into a former childlike self where one becomes weak, afraid, confused, and ineffective.

## Reference

Adler, A. (1964) *The Individual Psychology of Alfred Adler*. Harper Collins.

# 29 A Tennis Player Who Was Youngest in The Family and Who Took Pity on Weaker Opponents

I received a call from a mother of a 13-year-old nationally ranked male fencer who lived in Texas. She was distraught when seeing her son's matches because he would consistently lose to weaker players but would beat players that were ranked higher than him. The mother saw this pattern over and over but discussions and efforts to change the pattern by coaches did nothing to change it. Many years of training, money and the best coaching in America were put into his career, and out of desperation, the mother gave me a call. They had already tried standard sport psychology interventions like positive self-talk, encouragement, and positive reinforcement.

The young player presented as a shy and sensitive boy with the appearance of fear and fatigue. Fatigue is common in the overworked young athlete who has grown weary of all the travel and competitive grind. His shyness, sensitivity and depression were notable. He was raised by both parents and his older sibling was a girl 3 years his senior. The patient was a bright student who was getting A's in most of his subjects. In his first session he mentioned how cruel and abusive his father was and how the father would often beat his older sister. This would bring the patient to tears.

As we began our work, he remained soft-spoken and wary of me, but we managed to discuss some of the obvious strategies to remain focused and consistent no matter who the opponent happened to be. These cognitive interventions had some ameliorative effect, but the underlying tendency to lose matches to weaker opponents remained.

During one session he discussed losing a match in the finals to a weak player and as we spoke of the match, he mentioned that his opponent had a very mean, loud, aggressive, and demanding father and that my patient knew that if he won, his opponent's father would certainly unleash his wrath upon his son. My patient had observed his behavior in the past. I said that perhaps this was reminiscent of the way his own father had treated his older sibling and that maybe he was empathizing, sympathizing, and pitying this weak opponent and that he lost the match to protect him. The patient agreed with this interpretation, and we began to take note of this tendency. When insight like this occurs, one can begin to make conscious interventions including self-talk with the expectation that they will now take hold.

DOI: 10.4324/9781003272465-34

This patient was using the defense called Identification with the Victim. Anna Freud was the first to discuss this defense, a process whereby one sacrifices their own needs to protect another. In this case, the fencer defended against the guilt he would have felt in victory by letting his opponent win. The defense stemmed from the anguish that was elicited as he witnessed his sister being beaten by his dad.

Identification with the Victim was first described by Anna Freud and later expanded upon by Sandor Ferenczi (Fergusson and Gutierrez-Pelaez, 2022). Freud referred to it as altruistic surrender and considered it to be one of the two basic defenses. Ferenczi elaborated this defense and suggested that when one witnesses abuse, this terror becomes internalized, and one continues to be repeatedly victimized by it throughout life. Altruistic surrender and pitying your opponent are not adaptive defenses for competitive athletes.

We began to discuss the initial abuse he witnessed at home and created a new defense whereby he could manage any feelings of pity engendered during competition. When the awareness of his pity and its causes became known to him, we could begin to provide the standard behavioral suppressive techniques. When the unconscious dynamics are finally seen by the athlete, they are then able to employ the mental skill techniques that they have been taught. In this case the working through process included self-talk tips but always basing them upon the initial insight about pity and the pain he felt when his dad would beat his older sibling. This keeps the work alive, creative, and meaningful and thereby avoids the shallowness, superficiality, and repetitiveness so often seen in standard positive self-talk interventions.

## References

Freud, A. (1964) *The Ego and the Mechanisms of Defense*. International Universities Press.

Fergusson, A. and Gutierrez-Pelaez, M. (2022) *Sandor Ferenczi: A Contemporary Introduction*. Routledge.

# 30 The Influence of Twinship on Personality and Performance

When an athlete is a twin, they will benefit from this relationship and be faced with challenges as well. Being one of a pair guarantees that you will feel empathy for others and will probably become likable and socially skilled. However, twins often wind up feeling neglected or left out on occasion given the limited capacity of most parents.

The following is the case of a twin who was not living up to his potential in the ring and was losing bouts he should be winning in Tai Kwando. He was a 17-year-old high schooler who could have made it to the Olympics but because of this tendency to self-defeat, he never made it beyond Olympic trials. His parents knew that the time and money thus far invested would all be for naught if they did not fix this inhibition of function. As we explored the nature of his problem, we learned that he would become frozen, passive, and stiff in competition despite displaying excellent skill and fluidity in practice. In Tae Kwando you must be quick to respond in this lightning-fast sport and any hesitation or mental block leads to certain loss.

The uniqueness of this case was his birth order circumstances. He was a twin who arrived first, followed by his sister two minutes later. Like most first borns, he was perfectionist, hardworking, conscientious, and the more athletic of the pair, and his younger sister had learned to cope with this situation by becoming attention-seeking through temper tantrums thereby garnering most of the parental attention. These tantrums grew to the point of being traumatic for anyone who was unfortunate enough to witness them. This resulted in the parents telling my patient to set a good example and never provoke his sister. My patient eventually became the second fiddle to the sister. And by definition, second fiddles lose in the ring.

As we explored this dynamic in his history, the insight allowed him to understand how he might transfer this into matches by acting less than his opponents to avoid any violent tantrums. He had unconsciously learned to be the shadow of his sister and never to shine or stand out in any way, lest she start having a tantrum and scream. This unconscious trope that he was the shadow of his sister, dictated outcomes of matches by producing an unconscious avoidance of victory and thus failing to achieve his full potential.

DOI: 10.4324/9781003272465-35

This perception of being 'lesser than' became entrenched as he entered high school and he found himself befriending a peer who were narcissistic thus reinforcing his feeling of being 'second fiddle' and when he found himself in a class with his narcissistic friend, he would not be able to perform well during testing.

**Alfred Adler on birth order:** Adler believed that the family milieu is influenced by birth order and that the first born was more perfectionistic, disturbed, and conscientious, all to win back the undivided attention of the parents. The first born is thought to overcompensate for this loss of attention throughout their life.

The parents of this patient were educated and supportive of the analytic work and so we moved forward. The insight-oriented work was successful after we were able to connect his compulsion to lose with a childhood identity of being 'second fiddle'. This identity was reinforced in high school with his selection of a selfish, attention seeking, self-centered friend.

When sufficient insight was gained regarding his conflicts about winning, it was possible to establish a pregame, in-game, and post-game routine which allowed him to maintain focus and avoid self-defeat, owing to anxiety. This case shows how self-belief is established early in life and how conflicts about winning often determines one's ability to win or lose. It was only when insight was gained as to the cause of his freezing in the ring that he was able to effectively employ the standard performance enhancement techniques that are used in sport psychology. Insight must be gained if one hopes to break the cycle of losing. This case demonstrates the influence that being a twin has upon personality, choices in relationships, and attitudes about winning and losing.

## Reference

Adler, A. (1964) *Individual Psychology of Alfred Adler.* HarperCollins Publishers.

# Part VI

# Odds and Ends

This special section is included to clarify key issues including dream analysis, why athletes resist sport psychology, the psychology of injury, learning disabilities in the athlete, and what it's like to work with superstars.

DOI: 10.4324/9781003272465-36

# 31 An Athlete's Dream Analysis

Athletes have a variety of illuminating dreams, and they are usually willing, happy, and interested to keep track of them if asked to do so. Freud considered *The Interpretation of Dreams* his major work and his most valuable discovery. He revised the initial book eight different times which suggests how crucial this technique was to him. He often said the interpretation of dreams were the royal road to knowledge of the unconscious activities of the mind (1901).

Dream interpretation can uncover what is hidden and repressed within the athlete's unconscious and though the dream may seem strange, inconsequential, and incomprehensible at first, when time is spent on the dream analysis, the insight is invariably crucial. Each dream segment is a symbol that usually contains multiple meanings, feelings, and conflicts.

Dream interpretation is a threefold process which includes the reporting of the dream in all its details. When this is done, the athlete is asked to freely associate or discuss each of the dream segments. This will often show what the focal conflict is within the athlete. Phase three is the interpretation which is an intuitive process requiring a relaxed loose attention.

When a dream is interpreted correctly it usually feels 'right' to both patient and analyst and it provides a vivid image that will not be easily forgotten, and which can be referred to repeatedly.

There are models of dream analysis from various analytic schools of thought including object-relations theory, self-psychology, and information-processing theory and there is agreement now that dreams are attempts to integrate, synthesize and master deep rooted repressed and unresolved feelings and they do this primarily with images that hold and symbolize the feelings. Dreams are believed to be the minds attempt at mastering developmental problems, restoring self-esteem, resolving conflicts and contain conflicts that are heretofore unsettled.

Case study: This is a dream from a talented high school golfer who had recently given up on trying to overcome his putting yips. He had been expecting to play golf in college on the Division I level and was being actively recruited at the time, but he was suffering from the yips for over a year. He was a bright sensitive athlete who was quiet and shy and was doing

DOI: 10.4324/9781003272465-37

well in school. He described his mother as a kind and caring homemaker. His father was a successful surgeon, and the athlete described him as pessimistic. This is a dream that came shortly after his decision to give up on golf entirely, a sport that he had played since early childhood and a sport that he had obtained both acclaim and prestige.

**The golfer's dream:** This dream had two distinct parts and was introduced by the patient with the comment "This was the worst dream of my life." He was with his parents in a room he described as bland, and his mother approached him with a knife, and she had demonic eyes. She proceeded to stab him in the chest. He then noticed his father in the corner of the room and his father had a gun and shot his mother. In part two of this dream, he was with his friends the next day, and no one seemed to realize that his father had killed his mother or that she had stabbed him. He then left his friends and went into a room where he cried for five hours.

We discussed this dream in some detail and he sensed right away that it had something to do with his quitting golf. He was unable to associate productively to the first dream image of his mother stabbing him with a demonic look in her eyes. Often unsettling dream images are taken at face value by patients who assume that the characters in the dream represent real people or in this case that his mother represented his mother. We eventually came to realize that the mother image represented his dream of being a great golfer and that his dream had turned on him and killed him based upon his own anxiety. The patient was initially unable to associate to the image of the father shooting the mother, but we eventually came to realize this image was his own fury at failing to achieve his dream and this fury was turned inward and had a dangerous quality to it which we addressed so that he was not at risk for suicidal actions.

This dream demonstrates how the mind generates these stories which are fueled by unresolved and very intense emotions and when one takes the time to analyze them the patient finds answers to his emotional problems and finds relief. One of the many values of dream analysis is that the images are often vivid and can be referred back to time and again in order to work through the conflict or problem in question.

## Reference

Freud, S. (1901) *The Interpretation of Dreams* (Reprinted 1955). Basic Books.

# 32 Focus and Learning Problems in Athletes

I once asked an NFL football quarterback what was the biggest problem he faced as a quarterback, and he told me without hesitation "The players on my team cannot learn the playbook." Each week teams in the NFL are given a thick playbook which is over 200 pages and most of the players have trouble retaining the information. The quarterback went on to say that this failure to learn results in lost games. High-level sports are now based on numerous analytics and therefore require high-level cerebral capacity. I asked the quarterback if they had anyone on staff who addresses these learning problems, and he said no.

Bill Parcels, former coach of the New York Jets, would keep a baseball bat next to his easel as he spoke during team meetings. He did this to encourage the team to pay attention and to stay focused on what he was saying, but this threat of physical punishment seems like a primitive method at best.

Often when I work with a star athlete, I will provide lengthy analysis and progress reports monthly and when I ask if they read the report they tell me "Oh yeah, I think I scanned it last week." This usually means that in fact they did not even look at it. Even though playing a sport is understood to be physical, it also requires the athlete to listen and to learn each day and if there is some form of focus problem or learning disability, this will impact his career negatively.

There is psychoanalytic literature which suggests that the cause of many learning disabilities is rooted in childhood traumas (Gabbard, 1997). If there are family secrets, the child will quickly unlearn the ability to see. And if a gifted child has parents or teachers that harbor jealousy of their giftedness, the child will learn to shut off their brain, stop thinking and learn to become stupid. Jock culture disdains the egg head so if an athlete is exceptionally bright, they will slowly learn how to get stupid to avoid being ostracized.

The case presented here is of a professional tennis player's failure to learn a simple movement and how this failure had cost him dearly in lost earnings, status, and endorsement deals. The case demonstrates how his learning problem was dictated by a repetition compulsion, how we worked this

DOI: 10.4324/9781003272465-38

learning problem through, so that he eventually regained the ability to focus and learn which then helped him prosper in his athletic career.

This athlete had been my patient for eight years, and we had talked about many things over this time, ranging from his tennis woes all the way back to his childhood horrors. Over this time, he had been taught a variety of behavioral tools to help him to focus in tournaments yet he was still stuck in some ways. But an incident occurred that pushed his analysis into a deeper level and produced significant improvement in his athletic function. The patient came in to one session and remarked that he had lost his keys, a parapraxis we had seen a few times in the past.

**Parapraxis:** A parapraxis or Freudian slip, is defined as an error in speech, writing, or action that is based upon an unconscious interference of repressed thought or conflict within the personality. Freud believed that when a parapraxis occurred, it offered a window into the patient's unconscious.

I wondered aloud what losing his keys might mean and the patient insisted this was just an accident and denied any deeper meaning. A strong denial is often evidence of a reaction formation which means that the patient is defending against an emerging truth that threatens to be seen. I recalled for him how he had lost $100 last week by misplacing it and that one year ago, he had misplaced and lost $1,000. He grew heated at this and insisted that he had never misplaced $1,000 and I proceeded to show him evidence of this in my notes of a year ago.

As his denial continued, I suddenly realized that his 'lost' keys, his 'lost' money, and his 'lost' tennis matches reflected a bigger issue of his 'lost' childhood. This patient had no childhood to speak of since his mother died when he was very young, he was an only child, and his father was a depressed alcoholic who left shortly after he was born. He was then placed in foster care. I made the interpretation that his lost keys, lost money, and his lost matches were somehow a reflection of his lost childhood. He did not respond to this interpretation and the session ended unremarkably.

However, when the patient returned the following week, he began talking about how this week he suddenly remembered a basic aspect of his tennis stroke which for some reason he had never corrected. He told me that he realized that his grip had always been too tight but for some reason he could never remember to loosen it during matches. The result of this sudden insight and change of stroke was his first win on the tennis circuit.

He wondered aloud why he had not recalled such a basic aspect of his game. I then extended the interpretation, which was to connect his lost keys, his lost money, his losing in matches to his "lost childhood" and we spent the next several weeks working through this insight and his game improved markedly, all based upon this insight.

Many athletes carry the label of learning disabled, or attention deficit disorder and are handed some form of medication. However, often, the inability to learn something is psychological in nature and based upon being somehow stuck in their past.

The famous developmental psychologist Jean Piaget produced a theory which categorized a child's cognitive development into four stages including the sensory-motor stage, preoperational stage, concrete operations, and formal operations. It may be that some athletes are fixated at a certain stage of cognitive development based upon an emotional fixation, some form of serious unresolved loss from the past. They may still be in the pre-operational or concrete operational stage of thinking which means that no matter how many baseball bats, medications, and warnings you give, they cannot think, reason, recall, or learn as an adult. This case of the tennis player who finally learned how to learn is a case in point.

## References

Gabbard, G. (1997) *The Vicissitudes of Shame in Stage Fright In Work and its Inhibitions: Psychoanalytic Essays*, Eds, C. Socarides and S. Kramer. International Universities Press.

Piaget, J. (1976) *The Psychology of Intelligence. International Library of Psychology, Philosophy and Scientific Methods.*

# 33 The Psychological Causes of Sports Injuries

Injuries and accidents in sports are extremely costly to teams and to athletes. Statistics from 2015 show that MLB spent $700 million on salaries for injured players and the NFL spent $450 million on salaries for sidelined players. The NBA and the English Premier League both spent over $300 million on salaries of injured players. In addition, when starters are injured, the chances of a team making it to the playoffs diminish markedly. It is prudent to explore the psychological causes of injuries in sports. Usually, the causes of injury are reduced to explanations about overuse, fatigue, a misstep, or bad luck. But over the years, I have worked with many athletes who have been injured and I've had ample opportunity to observe the unconscious precursors to these injuries.

I believe the primary precursors of sport injury include 1) distraction from off-the-field stressors; 2) anger that has not been expressed; 3) the athlete's compulsive workaholism which leads to exhaustion and injury; 4) injury as secondary gain to escape the pain of competition, obtain rest, attention, and comfort; and 5) injury as a form of guilt or self-punishment. In this chapter I will discuss the fourth of these causes; secondary gain, although one could easily write an entire volume on these issues.

This is the case of a young golfer who broke his arm while rough housing with his girlfriend. I had met this 15-year-old boy to do an interview with him for a golf magazine. He had already gained national attention for his play and was a rising star. When I arrived at his home to interview him, I was greeted by his parents who escorted me to the living room where the boy was watching TV and I was surprised to see that his arm was in a cast. I recall the scene clearly because this was the day that O.J. Simpson was on the news in his effort the flee Los Angeles. The parents eventually left us in private and the first thing I asked was what happened to his arm. He said "Oh this. I was fooling around with my girlfriend last week and I fell and broke it." He smiled at me and then said "If you want to know the truth, I couldn't be happier. It's the first time in months that I get to stay home and not be on the road." I was a young sport psychologist then and his comment surprised me at the time. I had yet to become familiar with the grueling pace that young elite athletes must endure if they are to rise to the

DOI: 10.4324/9781003272465-39

top of their sport. Since then, I have learned to consider them young professionals that are not salaried but are living a professional life with a hectic schedule, little rest, constant travel, competitive play, and endless training.

So, is it any wonder that as they push their body in the extreme, the mind will eventually begin to demand that it get some rest? The rise toward fame is like a magnetic trap that seizes hold of them and is usually impossible to resist. Elite athletes often have the will power and defenses to suppress pain and exhaustion but inevitably the body collapses with an injury. And at times the injury is unconsciously wished for. And in this case the young golfer's injury allowed for rest, for escape from the stress of travel and competition and to gain some much-needed sympathy.

**The Secondary Gain of Injury:** Freud wrote about how an illness or injury can provide the sufferer with numerous benefits such as an escape from painful responsibilities and the gaining of sympathy. Freud considered secondary gain as one of the many reasons patients resist the cure since to resolve neurosis means to lose attention and sympathy (Freud, 1926).

A story of compulsive work, exhaustion, and the need to escape was seen with Tiger Woods. Here are two I personally observed. I recall seeing him on the range at Westchester Country Club in one of the few tournaments that he was not in contention. This made little difference to the mesmerized crowd who were ten-deep on the range watching him hit soaring 2 irons. After he finished hitting shots, the only way he managed to get to the clubhouse, which was 200 yards away, was to be surrounded by a contingent of eight uniformed bodyguards who shuffled their way through the throngs of fans and got him to the safety of the clubhouse in one piece. He was already at the level of a rock star. The next story came in 2002 at the US Open at Bethpage, New York. I followed Woods on day two as he was about to tee off on hole #10. He had to relieve himself, so he made his way to a green Portopotty near the tenth tee. He completed his bathroom functions and as he exited, the Portopotty was surrounded by at least five hundred fans that applauded him when he walked out. I knew then that he would somehow have to find a way to escape this absurd level of attention and adoration. But when you are earning upwards of $60 million a year in endorsements, it is hard to say no. He was trapped within his own fame and unable to walk away. He eventually resorted to acting out sexually with the probable unconscious intent to get caught and finally remove himself from the limelight, at least for a while. This is the secondary gain of accidents.

The young golfer I was interviewing on that day was beginning to get a taste of fame with press interviews, special country club privileges and peer group attention. He was already in a state of burnout from it all and he found a way out through injury.

Accidents do happen but often the accident is dictated by stressful conflicts the athlete is only vaguely aware of and is reluctant to verbalize. The reality is that agents, coaches, and fans are interested in seeing the athlete play, not rest. This leads the athlete into drug use, injury, or both. And the ever-present threat that one will be replaced within hours is seen every Monday in the NFL. If a football player is injured on a Sunday, he will be worked on Monday morning in the training room and he is acutely aware that at the same time, there will be three players on the practice field that morning trying out for his position. All this adds up to unrelenting stress. Supportive psychoanalytic therapy provides the athlete a chance to ventilate their emotions on a regular basis, so that costly injuries can be avoided, and so it can be determined whether they are pushing their body to the breaking point.

I have been interviewed many times by the media to discuss some recent psychological calamity in sport, be in Mike Tyson, Tiger Woods, or Michael Jordan. Invariably, the interviewer will be asking me about the athletes' pampered lifestyle, and how entitled they all are, and I will often respond by saying that the professional athletes' life is one of stress, hardship, pain, loneliness, and exhaustion. And to this I get blank stares.

The reality of all this is that money and fame pull the athlete into scenarios of overwork. Usually, the overwork is denied by all, and this inevitably leads to injury. The injury is either due to physical collapse or an unconscious decision to incur injury to escape the madness. In other words, Freudian slips occur not just verbally but physically as well.

## Reference

Freud, S. (1926) *Inhibitions, Symptoms, and Anxiety in Complete Psychological Works of Sigmund Freud*, Ed., J. Strachey. Norton.

# 34 Resistance to Sport Psychology

## What are Athletes so Afraid of?

Resistance is a primary concept in psychoanalysis and yet this problem is rarely mentioned in sport psychology textbooks. Resistance was first defined by Freud who noticed that patients would come late, miss sessions, or suddenly quit, based upon the fear of letting go of the past or fear of making change (Breuer and Freud, 1893–1895). Emergent mental health is often met with resistance, avoidance, and premature termination. The fact that resistance is not mentioned in standard sport psychology texts indicates that the field is in denial of this obvious problem.

"Techniques of Working with Resistance" edited by Milman and Goldman is the classic text on the subject and includes chapters by Sigmund Freud, Anna Freud, Heinz Kohut, Ralph Greenson, Peter Giovacchini, Robert Langs, and James Masterson. They approach the topic of why patients resist, owing to secondary gain, guilt, shame, and fear of dependency. Freud felt that ego defenses and transference caused some resistances which could be worked through with discussion. Id resistances or the repetition compulsions were more problematic and took considerable time to work through. Guilt or super ego resistance was deeper yet and took much time to work through.

In 2002 an intern and I published an article exploring the reason's athletes resist sport psychology by interviewing professionals, elite amateurs, and recreational athletes (Ferraro and Rush, 2002). We discovered that only about 10 percent had seen a sport psychologist, yet 80 percent felt that they would benefit from seeing one. These were competitive athletes who were playing golf, tennis, ran, swam, and played basketball or football. All were investing much time and money into their sport and rationalized their resistance by saying they had no time for sport psychology, sports were not that important to them, or they remarked that they were not crazy. We concluded that the reasons for not seeing a sport psychologist were largely unconscious and included the athlete's tendency to use action to ward off feelings. This tendency towards alexithymia accounted for the large-scale resistance among them, despite apparent need for help. They would much prefer to suffer in silence and fail rather than talk about what was troubling them. We found that athletes will often cope with their underlying anxiety

DOI: 10.4324/9781003272465-40

by resorting to superstitious behaviors (like wearing a certain kind of sock), using performance enhancing drugs, or by eating certain kinds of foods.

My own practice shows that 50% of athletes drop out within 6 sessions which is long before they have been helped. The reason for this notable finding is multi-determined. Some fantasize that the cure would be instantaneous and easy and resistance hits when they see that this work will require that they talk about personal matters, and this frightens many athletes.

**A case study on resistance.** A fifteen-year-old high school lacrosse star is brought to my office with complaints of intense pregame anxiety, which included nausea, vomiting, sleeplessness, butterflies, tension, and worry. This had been going on for three years and was now getting worse as Division I colleges started to recruit him. Resolving his issue was crucial because his performance was flat and the potential to gain lucrative scholarships worth as much as $300,000 was at risk.

Intake revealed inhibition of aggression on the field, hyper perfectionism, and lowered self-esteem as well as chronic anxiety and self-doubt while playing. This is a typical case of young talent with demanding parents, intense training by harsh coaches and overwhelming attention, all of which were flooding and overcoming this youngster's still immature defenses. Our work lasted three sessions during which time I systematically provided support, empathy, and guidance in the form of articles I have published in this area, as well as ways to reduce anxiety. The case was suddenly terminated with a phone call by the parents with no explanation. This is a common experience for sport psychologists, and it is often difficult to understand what caused the resistance. It may be that he was becoming too assertive at home, it may be that he realized that the work would involve talking about underlying feelings which he would rather not do. It may be that someone found out he was in therapy, and it produced shame in him. It may be that the athlete or the parents had a fantasy that I had some sort of magic I would wave and "voila, all fixed" in a jiffy. Or perhaps it was an economic factor with a refusal to invest in the working of the mind. All these factors are in play and can easily derail the best efforts by a sport psychologist.

A good dissertation for a young grad student in this area is to research resistance to sport psychology in athletes and coaches. Resistance is the most common issue in the field and research is needed to understand this. The therapist must find a balance between establishing a safe working alliance which is non-threatening and offer interventions which the athlete can use on the field. At the same time, one must educate the athlete, the parents, and the coach about the underlying dynamics that are unconscious and that will resist exposure.

## References

Breuer, J. and Freud, S. (1893–1895) *Studies in Hysteria*, Standard Edition 2. Hogarth Press, 1955.

Ferraro, T. and Rush, S. (2002) Why Athletes Resist Sport Psychology. *Journal of Athletic Insight.*

Milman, D. and Goldman, G. (1987) *Techniques of Working with Resistance*. Jason Aronson.

# 35 The Self-Conscious Golfer Unable to Handle Fame

This 14-year-old golfer came to me with symptoms of profound self-consciousness, anxiety and obsessive-compulsive behaviors including checking to see if she had stains on her blouses and checking to see if her hair was in place as she walked through school. She was a blonde, extremely attractive, and well-developed girl who had already achieved some measure of national fame. Her father felt she was not performing up to potential and hoped I would help her improve her performance woes.

During matches she was extraordinarily anxious and painfully distracted when spectators were watching her. Her good looks insured that many people would be enjoying her game as well as the look of her young body in motion. It was as she had become trapped within the novel "Lolita" (Nabokov, 1955) and did not know how she got there or what to do about it. She admitted to me she enjoyed the admiration and attention she received when she walked around or when she played golf but also dreaded the feelings of anxiety and the need to maintain a façade of perfection.

We used a variety of interventions to settle her anxiety and improve her focus and these things had some impact on her game only because she seemed to appreciate the chance to come to the office and ventilate her anxieties. She said she was a constant disappointment to her father who was very volatile and often embarrassing to her when he would shout out unpredictably.

I began to formulate some of the reasons for her anxiety. About six months into our work, she came to the office in a near panic. She told me she was exhausted from having to press her clothing for 45 minutes every day before going to school and it was taking her far too long doing her hair, choosing her clothes, and putting on makeup. I asked her about this compulsive behavior and told her I was thinking it had something to do with the father's volatility but as we talked, she had a more accurate and profound interpretation of this compulsive behavior. She said the compulsive behavior had more to do with when she was in 6th grade, was a tomboy, wore sloppy clothes and didn't look very good. But by 7th grade she reached puberty and began to change in appearance, developed a nice figure, and started to gain lots of attention, owing not only to her golf game

DOI: 10.4324/9781003272465-41

but also to her good looks. She began to feel trapped by this attention and felt she must maintain an extreme effort to maintain it by looking perfect and playing perfect golf. She said she did not want to lose the nice attention but the effort to keep it was ridiculously arduous. She referred to this process as "glowing up."

I asked her what "glowing up" meant, and she said it was a new term kids use when you suddenly change for the better and grow up into someone different and better than before, like the butterfly and cocoon metaphor. She went on to say that for her "glowing up" was both good and bad. She had struck upon the essential problem of fame and what occurs to many athletes I work with. It is as if the fame consumes and entraps them, and they do not have the ego strength, self-identity, and defensive system to manage the attention. What occurs is that they often develop the mid-range defense of overcontrol with desperate efforts to manage it with a variety of compulsive behaviors. In her case, it was now centered on an hour-and-a-half of clothing preparation.

There are many cases like this where a young athlete achieves fame and then seems wholly unable to handle it. In the film "Yesterday" directed by Peter Boyle, an agent has a chat with a newly discovered talent and says to him "Tell me you're ready to drink from the poisoned chalice of fame and fortune." This scene is notable because it reveals the truths about fame, a thing that is frequently poisonous enough to kill you. I have worked with young athletes who have lost all sense of who they are upon experiencing global fame. And the results are they will often turn to drugs to settle themselves down.

If we think of this issue in Piagetian terms, we will ask how you get someone to move out of the assimilation process and into the accommodation process (Piaget, 1967). For a developing athlete, the question then is, how does one help them to accommodate to newfound levels of attention and success? How to help them get comfortable at this next level of functioning, competitively, emotionally, psychologically, and socially. If the NFL had answers to this question, it would save them hundreds of thousands of dollars each year in the rookies that fail and flame out. Unfortunately, Piaget's work focused primarily on cognitive development and not competitive development.

We can also turn to the Jungian concept of liminal space in the effort to have athletes accommodate to a higher status (Jung, 1956). Jung borrowed the concept of liminal space from ancient rituals where clans would take "initiates" who reached the age of puberty out into the forest for a few months where they would be trained and prepared to move into the next station in life. The liminal space consists of many rituals which gave the initiates time to learn and to accept their new status and they would have mentors who would counsel them, reinforce their new status and its new responsibilities. Currently we do not have any of these liminal rituals which help athletes to prepare to accommodate to their new status. So instead, we hear phrases like "glowing up" which is the younger generations way of expressing this process but without the means or the support to do so. The result is a "blowing up" rather than a "glowing up."

## References

Jung, C. (1956) *Symbols of Transformation (Collected Works of C.G. Jung, Vol.* 5). Princeton University Press.

Nabokov, V. (1955) Lolita. Olympia Press

Piaget, (1967) *The Psychology of Intelligence.* International Library of Psychology, Philosophy and Scientific Method

# 36 What it's Like to Work with A Super Star and The Problem of Countertransference

The working alliance, transference and countertransference insights are among the foundational tools of depth sport psychology and what differentiates it from standard sport psychology. Traditional sport psychology relies almost exclusively on technical and mechanistic interventions aimed at teaching the athlete ways to suppress unruly emotions. The basic tenet of this book has been to demonstrate how suppressive techniques alone will not be sufficient and that more is needed. The use and the interpretation of the therapeutic relationship is a core principle of depth sport psychology and gives the treatment its curative power.

The therapeutic relationship consists of the working alliance, transference, and counter- transference. The working alliance is defined as the good will and cooperation that is created in the patient based upon the therapist's non-judgmental and empathic efforts. Transference is the perceptual distortion that the patient brings to the relationship and finally countertransference is the perceptual distortion in the therapist based upon his reactions to the patient.

The case about to be presented involves my work with a very well-known athlete and I will be discussing the issue of my countertransference, something rarely written about in the literature.

Nearly every sport psychologist is a former athlete, and most are sport fans. And when you get a chance to work with a star athlete, it produces the natural tendency to be in some awe of them. This is what we call subjective counter-transference issues. Countertransference can be a powerful tool while working with athletes, but it can also produce errors in the way one manages them.

Countertransference was first described by Freud who defined it as those emotional and physical reactions to the patient's behaviors or distorted perceptions (Stefano, 2015). Over the years, countertransference has been used as a therapeutic tool, helping the analyst to understand the underlying dynamics of the patient, how they distort and do damage to relationships

DOI: 10.4324/9781003272465-42

and how to avoid falling into those pitfalls while working with the patient. If the therapist can assess how they are made to feel in the presence of a patient, they are well on their way to understanding the patient's personality, maladaptive behaviors and are in a far better position to provide insight and to avoid therapeutic problems.

In sport psychology there is little mention of countertransference but to his credit, Mark Anderson wrote about his countertransference despite having no apparent psychoanalytic training. He edited a standard text on sport psychology and included a chapter by himself, entitled "Touching Taboos: Sex and the Sport Psychologist". He discussed the counter-transference pertaining to sexual attraction while working with the athlete (Anderson, 2005). But that remains the only reference I could find on this subject in the current sport psychology literature.

An instance of an overly positive counter-transference problem was seen in the case of Marilyn Monroe and her treating psychiatrist, Dr. Ralph Greenson. He was a world renowned and respected analyst who worked in Beverly Hills and treated many of Hollywood's stars. He undertook the analysis of Marilyn Monroe and was apparently so enamored with her sweet charm, incredible magnetism, and beauty that he would often ask her to his home after sessions where she would have drinks and interact with his family. We all know of the outcome of this case when she suicided of an overdose of pills prescribed by him.

A case of excellent management of countertransference was seen with Phil Jackson, the coach of the Chicago Bulls of the NBA when he was faced with managing Michael Jordan. When Jordan joined the Chicago Bulls, Phil Jackson understood that Jordan's talent and star quality would present challenges to himself and the team members. Jackson's ability to remain in charge, neutral and fair to all, enabled the team to win six NBA championships. I would suggest that it is rare for coaches to manage their counter-transference reactions to star players. I recall having a meeting with a coach upon the arrival of a soccer super star and how we attempted to address this issue. Stars bring gifts but also challenges to any team.

In this chapter I will discuss the challenges of countertransference I faced while working with a superstar figure skater.

Most super stars develop what we call Acquired Situational Narcissism which is the inevitable attitude of entitlement which comes as they experience constant adoration, expensive gifts, and privileges from virtually every human they interact with. As a typical example of how narcissism develops, I will tell you a personal story. My family owned many thoroughbred racehorses, so growing up I got to know many super star jockeys. One of them had just returned from a race in Saudi Arabia where he rode one of the sheikh's horses and won. Not only did the jockey get paid a huge amount for the win but he told me the sheikh also gave his wife a diamond, ruby, and sapphire necklace worth $250,000. When you receive treatment like this, it does something to you. What it does is produce Acquired Situational Narcissism in the athlete. After Gwyneth Paltrow won her second Academy Award, she casually and smartly remarked "This much attention is not healthy for anyone."

Another one of my patients went to a European awards ceremony to receive an honor and while she was in the back room waiting to go on stage, she was seated with some of the world's best male soccer players, including Ronaldinho, Cristiano Ronaldo, and Lionel Messi. When she returned home, I asked her what her thoughts were about it and she remarked "When I looked at these guys, I got the impression they had never heard the word no." Stars rarely if ever hear the word no. So, when you work with a super star, holding the therapeutic frame and remaining neutral is an enormous challenge.

The first call from a super star is memorable. In the case I will now discuss, her agent found me by reading a piece I had done on methods of treating self-defeat in the athlete. The agent explained that his client was an LPGA player who was formerly ranked #4 in the world but was demonstrating a pattern of self-defeat.

I began my work with this player by taking a history, allowing her to ventilate and by doing some here and now interventions about forgiveness, pacing and focus. Over the first year of our work, her slump was resolved, and she returned to the top of her field. Throughout this period, my countertransference feelings fluctuated. On one level, I obtained pleasure by seeing her do well and it was easy to enjoy our work together. Our working alliance had been formed and was going well.

**The Working Alliance:** The working alliance is what Freud referred to as the friendly and affectionate aspects of the work which would be a vehicle to success in the analysis. By taking serious interest in the patient and their issues, Freud felt this would bond the patient to the work and allow for the more arduous work to take place. A vast literature on this subject suggests that the emotional quality of the relationship between therapist and patient is more highly correlated with outcome than any other specific factor (Strupp, 1989). Despite this fact, surprisingly little has been written about the working alliance between the athlete and the sport psychologist except for a few pages in *Clinical Sport Psychology* by Gardner and Moore (2005.) The working alliance is established and maintained with an air of playfulness, openness, respect, and an overall relaxed and casual demeanor as the sessions unfold.

But as I worked with this super star, our work felt increasingly superficial, even boring. Furthermore, there was never mention or acknowledgement of what we had been doing despite a sizable increase in earnings and a gain in world ranking. In addition, sessions were being missed regularly. I explained that missed sessions would be charged but at her level of income, this was of small concern. These missed appointments were an expression of open disregard for our work and for me and my time. The failure to acknowledge gains was also a demonstration that I was superfluous to her gains. These are all predictable countertransference feelings when working with narcissists and it is crucial to be aware of them so that one does not become angry or depressed over it. It takes a very long time to work these projections through with the narcissist.

Serious acting out occurred about 18 months after we started work and she once again began to manifest the same kind of self-defeat that prompted her agent to call me in the first place. She would get into accidents, lose events, start to dabble in drugs, and act out socially in such a way that her endorsements were in jeopardy. These are standard manifestations of the self-destructive nature of the narcissist athlete who is desperately seeking ways of avoiding loneliness, boredom, and emptiness either chemically or by misbehaviors which they consider to be stimulating.

This case is ongoing, but my intent was to demonstrate how countertransference with the star athlete is powerful and it takes great patience and skill to manage it properly. The countertransference is an intermingling of both positive feelings in the therapist based upon the fame of the athlete but that soon gets mixed with negative countertransference as disregard and disrespect for the therapist emerges. The only way to properly manage this is to understand the feelings being experienced and to share them with the patient.

## References

Anderson, M. (2005) Touching Taboos: Sex and the Sport Psychologist. In Ed. M. Anderson, *Sport Psychology in Practice*. Human Kinetics.

Stefano, A. (2015) The Origins of Countertransference. *The Psychoanalytical Review*, 102(14): 437–460.

Strupp. H. (1989) Psychotherapy: Can the Practitioner learn from the Researcher? *American Psychologist*, Vol. 44: 717.

Gardner, F. and Moore, Z. (2005) *Clinical Sport Psychologist*. Human Kinetics.

# Part VII

# Conclusion

Concluding remarks and a look at how Depth Sport Psychology provides the perfect rubric for the long-term psychological work that is needed within this field.

DOI: 10.4324/9781003272465-43

# 37 The Coming Paradigm Shift in Sport Psychology

Depth Sport Psychology rests upon the basic assumption that athletes have an unconscious that often dictates athletic outcomes based upon conflicts, and inhibitions that they are not even aware of. Standard Sport Psychology rejects the very idea of an unconscious and as a result, they are stuck in the self-limiting position of trying to fix present current problems through persuasion, cajoling and the hope that pushing a positive psychological agenda will have some impact on the athlete. This has proven to be an ineffective and weak approach.

Most work with athletes center upon the psychology of anxiety, anger, or focus. These emotions are strong enough to destabilize the mind as well as the body and sport psychology is assigned the task of addressing these emotional and cognitive states. Athletes and coaches often hold the fantasy that fixing anxiety or anger is quick and easy and standard sport psychology has responded to this fantasy by agreeing and promising that positive self-talk and deep breathing, visualization and goal setting will do the trick. Sadly, this has proven to be a falsehood.

In this book, I have tried to demonstrate the richness offered with the variety of psychoanalytic theories developed over the past 120 years based upon the position that our unconscious holds most of the causes of our anguish and its techniques are designed to penetrate into the inner recesses of the mind to resolve our pain. These psychoanalytic theories can be used with athletes and it is no mystery why they have been avoided thus far in sports. Man's defensive strategies are all designed to deny the power of the unconscious and Freud himself understood that his techniques would be feared and ridiculed. But though the analytic process may be arduous, the payoff is large. I hope that this book has demonstrated this.

The theories of Sigmund Freud tell us that the mind of the athlete is deep and that exploring just the surface of the mind leaves behind the most influential areas. The athletes' unconscious guilt, self-concept, primitive defenses, and dream life all impact play and no amount of denial on the part of coaches, players or psychologists will change that. It is also astounding to

DOI: 10.4324/9781003272465-44

me that outside of articles by Fenichel (1939), Deutsch (1999), and Dervin (1999), psychoanalysis has not shown any real interest in sports or the athlete.

Adler's work on overcompensation, and birth order, Mahler's work on separation anxiety, Jungian liminal space, and Freud's discussion of repetition compulsions all beg for more research and discussion. In this book I have briefly introduced the various psychoanalytic techniques including free association, working alliance, dream analysis, the study of defenses, resistance analysis, transferences, and counter transference as they apply to the athlete. The area of team dynamics was only touched upon in my chapter on regression in groups, a concept which was started by Freud and developed by Wilfred Bion. Emotions such as envy, jealousy, shame are the special domain of psychoanalysis starting with the work of Melanie Klein. These theories have the potential to provide great insight for the embattled coaches and G.M.s who struggle to fix the infighting and unrest found in most locker rooms.

The field of sport psychology has stagnated and is at an impasse largely because of its refusal to acknowledge the athlete's unconscious. The learning paradigms of Skinner, Pavlov and Watson showed promise with the introduction of classical and operant conditioning models of human behavior. But you can only go so far with reinforcement theory when you have an unconscious that works in secret and drives towards self-defeat. You can use all the reinforcement you like but the demons of one's past have a way of defeating the best laid plans of a behavior modifier. As the saying goes "you may be through with the past but the past ain't through with you."

As Thomas Kuhn mentioned in "The Nature of Scientific Revolutions", paradigm shifts are always resisted but are inevitable and necessary if a field is to grow.

The future will find the field of sport psychology using both suppressive interventions so popular nowadays but will also include treatment of the athlete's unconscious defenses, underlying conflicts, repressed traumas, unresolved losses, and dreams that are pressing for expression.

There is nothing more fascinating then work with world class athletes. They have an unconscious that must be dealt with. Contrary to what is a basic tenet in sport psychology that athletes are paragons of mental health, they are just like the rest of us, suffer just as much as we do if not more and they too self-defeat when you least expect it. In an unusually unguarded moment this is what one world class athlete recently said to me "Why can't people understand that I am a regular person who happens to have one very well-developed craft. Other than that, I'm the same as them. Why do they expect me to be so much more?"

Most athletes are phallic types with displays of self-assurance, arrogance, aggression, energy and leadership ability and this attitude of invincibility serves them well in sports, a profession that requires strength, bravery, and self-assurance (Reich, 1945). But the athlete's character and the character of sport is defensive in nature, and it requires great skill to work with them effectively to establish trust and safety and to get into the deeper issues which are actively destroying their success.

One of Western literature's greatest motifs is the quest for the Holy Grail. The first version, written by Chrétien de Troyes in 1190, is about Perceval, a knight who is assigned the task of finding a grail which will provide healing energy and health to an ailing king whose land has grown fallow. The grail, like a trophy, is symbolized as a chalice. There have been many versions of this tale told throughout the past 1,000 years through novels, music, poetry, and film. The grail is always described as a hidden object and the knight will need faith, perseverance, focus, and courage in order to find it.

This tale parallels the work in sport psychology. The athlete's powers have grown weak, and their careers have grown fallow and the Holy Grail that I must help them to find remains hidden inside their unconscious. The therapeutic work involves a journey taken by us both into the forest of their inner mind where the answers lie. When we are successful, they are released from their stupor and begin to feel energy and power once again. The journey produces epiphanies. Many athletes resist this effort but for those who engage in this process, their conflicts are uncovered and resolved, their energy returns as does their ability to win.

The domain of Depth Sport Psychology opens up unchartered areas in the world of sports including understand the dynamics of gamesmanship, the dangers and challenges of fame, the common occurrence of Situational Acquired Narcissism, permission to feel power and aggression, a return to the ability to enjoy sports based upon sublimation, the unconscious dynamic of guilt and self-defeat. Depth Sport Psychology offers many benefits to the athlete including the opportunity to be listened to carefully, to be able to ventilate, gains in forgiveness and self-esteem, and the problem solving of complex personal issues. And perhaps the most valued lesson of all is the chance to be accompanied on a journey within which most of the answers to one's anguish are to be found. The past is the domain of Depth Sport Psychology, and for sport psychology to remain relevant and to grow, back to the future it must go, into the inner sanctums of the mind and back to the very foundations of psychology and to the theories of the unconscious first discovered by one of the great thinkers of the 20th Century, Sigmund Freud.

## References

Dervin, D. (1999) Sports, Athletes, and Games in a Psychoanalytic Perspective. In *Mind-Body Games*. Taylor & Francis.

de Troyes, Chrétien. (1190). *Percival, the Story of the Grail* (trans. B. Raffel, 1990). Yale University Press.

Deutsch, H. (1999) A Contribution to the Psychology of Sport. In *The Therapeutic Process, the Self and Female Psychology*. Routledge.

Fenichel, O. (1939) The Counter-Phobic Attitude. *The International Journal of Psychoanalysis*, Vol. 20: 263.

Kuhn, T. 1962. *The Structure of Scientific Revolutions*. The University of Chicago Press.

Reich, W. 1945. *Character Analysis*. Simon & Schuster.

# Index

Made in the USA
Monee, IL
13 September 2026

62977683R00087